WE ARE NOT BROKEN

GEORGE M. JOHNSON

LITTLE, BROWN AND COMPANY

New York   Boston

Copyright © 2021 by George M. Johnson

Cover art copyright © 2021 by Johnalynn Holland. Cover design by
Karina Granda. Cover copyright © 2021 by Hachette Book Group, Inc.

Little, Brown and Company
Hachette Book Group
1290 Avenue of the Americas, New York, NY 10104

Visit us at LBYR.com

First Edition: September 2021

Little, Brown and Company is a division of Hachette Book Group,
Inc. The Little, Brown name and logo are trademarks of
Hachette Book Group, Inc.

The publisher is not responsible for websites (or their content)
that are not owned by the publisher.

Photographs courtesy of George M. Johnson

Library of Congress Cataloging-in-Publication Data
Names: Johnson, George M. (George Matthew), 1985– author.
Title: We are not broken / George M. Johnson.
Description: First edition. | New York : Little, Brown and
Company, 2021. | Audience: Ages 12 & up. | Summary: "This is a
memoir of George's boyhood in New Jersey, growing up with their
brother and two cousins, all under the supervision of their larger-
than-life grandmother"— Provided by publisher.
Identifiers: LCCN 2020051559 | ISBN 9780759554603 (hardcover) |
ISBN 9780759554610 (ebook) | ISBN 9780759554627 (ebook other)
Subjects: LCSH: African American gay men—New Jersey—
Biography. | African American boys—New Jersey—Biography. |
African American families—New Jersey—Biography.
Classification: LCC HQ76.27.A37 J646 2021 |
DDC 306.76/6208996073—dc23
LC record available at https://lccn.loc.gov/2020051559

ISBNs: 978-0-7595-5460-3 (hardcover), 978-0-7595-5461-0 (ebook)

Printed in the United States of America

LSC-C

Printing 1, 2021

This book is dedicated to

Louise Kennedy Evans Elder,

the woman who my cousins and I affectionately called Nanny. My grandmother, our
matriarch, our friend. Nanny, you gave all of
yourself to us at many points, at the expense
of your own health. As cancer attacked your
body six different times over the span of forty
years, you never lost your unwavering belief
in God and the afterlife. Although your body is
no longer in the physical world, we know that
your spirit lives on—"death" isn't real, and you
are still with us as a new form of life. May your
many lessons live through us so that we may
be a gift to future generations, just as you
were to us while here on this earth.

Author's Note

Tamir Rice was twelve years old when he was killed by police officers who mistook his toy gun for a real one. It's a story that's all too familiar. I, too, was a Black boy who played with toy guns. My cousins Rall and Rasul and my little brother, Garrett, were Black boys who played with toy guns. All four of us got "the speech" early on about how unsafe it was for us to do the same things as our white friends. It was a reminder of the danger in our simple existence.

Black boys don't have it easy in American society. We face many systems of oppression that tend to harden us, forcing us to lock in our emotions and exist in a state of near-constant internal rage. These systems become pipelines to our trauma—pipelines that many of us never make it out of. Though this trauma and adversity often beat down our spirits, we may be bruised, but we are not broken.

We Are Not Broken is a window into the lives of Lil'

Rall, Rasul, Garrett, and I—four Black boys growing up in the small city of Plainfield, New Jersey, under the supervision of our grandmother Nanny. We were four imaginative kids who were allowed the freedom to be individuals and the agency to make decisions rather than be told there was only one way. Centered on our adolescence, these stories discuss masculinity, racism, religion, violence, Blackness, and, most importantly, Black joy. In addition, these stories journey into Black womanhood and the narrative of the Black grandmother—a figure that has often been the cornerstone of progress and love in our community.

This book also contains heavy messages around corporal punishment, mass incarceration, racism, anti-Blackness, and homophobia. There is strong language, including the words "nigga" and "faggot." When reading this book, please refer to the words as the n-word or the f-word, especially if you are non-Black or if you are non-Queer, respectively.

Black boys in society are often seen as adults by the age of twelve. We are viewed as dangerous and more prone to violence, and often left broken. This book is an attempt to change our narrative and give voice to our stories through our own eyes. Most importantly, this is an opportunity to disprove any notion that Black boys don't deserve love, affection, care, and the space to be open, vulnerable, emotional, and kind.

Many places around the world are now in a state of protest over the police-caused deaths of Tony McDade, Breonna Taylor, George Floyd, and countless others. George Floyd was once a Black boy. Many Black men were once Black boys, and this is our story of survival in a world that has rarely seen our beauty.

Introduction

"All shut eyes ain't sleep."

> The most disrespected person in America is the Black woman. The most unprotected person in America is the Black woman. The most neglected person in America is the Black woman. —*Malcolm X*

I've probably come across this quote more than a thousand times on social media, television, or even on the radio. As someone who has multiple identities, with being Black and Queer at the top of that list, I recognize the feeling of living in a society that sees you as disposable. I understand what it's like to put so much into a world that requires you to save it. A world that never once gave a second thought about saving you. Still, being a Black woman is a unique experience, one I could never fully understand—much like my own unique experience with Blackness and Queerness.

I come from a family of strong Black women. My mother, my aunts, my grandmothers, and their mothers were all women who led their families, supported one another, and stepped in to handle family business without needing to be asked. Black women have always been the ones expected to heal us and make us whole, often neglecting to take the time to heal themselves.

The Black woman who sat at the center of our universe was my mother's mother, who the grandchildren affectionately called Nanny. When people say, "We rest on the shoulders of giants," this woman comes to my mind immediately. In her life, she was most certainly disrespected but didn't take no shit. Oftentimes she was probably unprotected, which is why she usually carried a weapon. I know there were many times she was neglected, yet she never once neglected the duties she felt were her purpose as our grandmother. This story is a way to love, honor, and care for her in a way that the world never has.

Louise Kennedy Evans was her birth name; she was born in March 1941 in Spartanburg, South Carolina. She was the tenth child of thirteen kids born to my great-grandmother Lulu Mae Evans. When Nanny was a little girl, her family's house caught on fire. Her three youngest siblings all passed away, making her the "baby" of the family. Even as the baby, she had something special about her, something domineering and omnipresent. As the youngest to survive, she was left here for a reason. She was left here to change the world, and that she did.

Caregiving came naturally to her. She had my mother, Kaye, when she was only sixteen years old, and dropped out of school around the tenth grade before marrying my grandfather Rall Elder and starting her family. She would go on to have an additional three kids by birth—Rall L. Elder Jr., Sarah Elder, and Stephanie Elder (who we call Aunt Munch). She also had one adopted nephew—my uncle Kevin Hobson— and raised twenty-four foster kids over the years for the state of New Jersey. She would go by many names in her life: Mommy, Lou, Louise, Aunt Lou, Big Lou, Ms. Elie, Irene, Nanny, and several others. That's the kind of spirit she had. The embodiment of every woman. A reflection of all.

Nanny worked hard for each dollar she ever earned. At every point in her life she had some kind of hustle going on. She held down regular jobs, including one working as a registered nurse; she owned a daycare; she did flea marketing; and she ran a catering business for many years. She had other side hustles, including my favorite—providing microloans to the women in her church. With the loans, the women would buy diamonds from Mrs. Ruth, the diamond lady in our neighborhood, and pay her back at a low interest rate. Nanny kept a little red book in which she detailed all the money she was owed, and used it to track payments. She was that type of boss.

With all she had going on, though, her greatest investment was in her grandkids, or, as she would say, "the grands." We got the most of her time, love, and energy, something none of us will ever forget. Nanny always used to say the world was playing a trick on her because she kept having grandsons. First my cousins Lil' Rall and Lil' Kevin in 1980, then my cousin Rasul in 1981, me in 1985, my younger brother, Garrett, in 1988, and my cousin Justice in 1994. She desperately wanted a granddaughter, but with me, an effeminate boy who spent the most time with her, I think she got a little bit of what she wanted. Still, she would have to wait nearly twenty-five years after her first grandchild was born before our little cousin Kennedy Elder-Law arrived in 2004. Kennedy was sort of named after Nanny, with Nanny's middle name being her first name. Nanny got to live her final years with a granddaughter as her sidekick and best friend. Although, in our own way, each of us felt we held the title of her bestie. But that's the magic of the Black family dynamic. People in our family don't just use son, daughter, cousin, or grandmother as a placeholder. We do the work to actually become friends.

I want to be clear when I say, you don't grow up in a home with a Black grandmother where wisdom isn't being shared on a daily basis. Nanny was no different. She was the Black matriarch who told it like it was and always meant what she said. When she talked, the ancestors spoke through her. Her body was the vessel for the wisdoms of a thousand Black grandmothers over several millennia, with word-of-mouth truths passed down over generations, crossing oceans and being adapted.

When I watch movies that have that Black-woman wisdom, I instantly think about her. When Cicely Tyson did one of her majestic monologues. Or when Loretta Devine or Jennifer Lewis gives us one of those infamous rants on how "if we knew better, we would do better." Or anytime I read the texts of Angela Davis, Audre Lorde, Nikki Giovanni, and the mighty Toni Morrison. I'm immediately enveloped in their words, the warmth, the Blackness. It's the same warmth I felt each time my grandmother scolded me and molded me, and a feeling I think we all share.

Nanny always used to say, "The things I didn't get right with my kids, I tried my hardest to get right with my grandkids." The lengths she went to—to ensure that we had the best of everything—are a testament to how she truly was a woman of her word. Her word was her bond. Of course, no one ever gets everything right, but for a woman who defied the odds since childhood, she came damn close to getting it right with all of us.

Sometimes I have this vision—a vision of four little Black boys lying in the bed, sleeping after a long day of bike rides and video games. Four heads sticking out from underneath the covers at the top of the bed. The moonlight streaming through the window, illuminating the room. Nanny comes into view, walking up the hallway, peeking in to make sure that we are okay before she finally goes to bed. I imagine what she was thinking in that moment. How beautifully the moonlight danced on our skin. How, although we gave her hell every day, having us with her still felt like heaven. Wondering who we would turn out to be when we got older. Wondering if the words and lessons she gave us, day in and day out, would be remembered.

I often think about the power of the Black word, the way we've passed down traditions since the beginning of time. I consider how our ancestors' words and thoughts were created during such different times but remain relevant for every period that we, as their descendants, enter. *You can't know where you are going if you don't know where you have been*, as the ancestors would say. Nanny knew where we had been, but not just in our own lives. She was the connection of old to new. The oracle of our family. The gateway to the past, just as the Black women before her had been. And as much as she ensured our care in the present, she also knew that there would be a time when she would no longer be with us in the physical world.

After Nanny passed, all of us wondered, *What will we do next?* Who would be the person to guide us as a family? Who would be the tiebreaker and the decision maker for us moving forward? Who would we come to when we needed to hear the Word of God? But that's why she left us something more important than her recipes, or money, or jewelry. She left us with the words.

Her "Nannyisms"—the little quips of wisdom that my family has lived on for generations, her small reminders of life lessons—will guide each story in this book. *All shut eyes ain't sleep* was one of her sayings, and it meant that when you think folks ain't around or paying attention, they really are. Nanny, although your eyes may be shut in this physical world, we know that our queen ain't slept a wink. Since you moved on to your next phase of life, you have been above us, wielding your power of protection and blessings in so many ways. You've been protecting us from the other side, just as you did on Earth. I can still feel you some days. There are times when I dream and you come through as clear as day, still helping me from the other side. There are times when we see a ladybug—oh, how you loved your ladybug pins on your church dresses—and we know you are with us at that very moment. Or the times when I mention your name and I get a chill, letting me know you are in the room.

We quote the famous ancestors so much that we tend to forget about the ones we had in our everyday lives. Nanny, this book is a love letter to the Black boy joy you created, the Black-woman experience, your powerful lessons and words, and you—the Black grandmother that saved generations.

It's now time for the world to blessed by the greatest storyteller ever known. We will always have your words, and we know that your word is our bond.

1

My Cousins. My Brothers.

Nannyism: "You gotta bring ass to get ass."

I don't remember when my little brother, Garrett, and I first met our cousins, because they're woven into my earliest memories. There was no introduction of "Meet Lil' Rall and Rasul" because they have always been part of my existence. They were my protectors, my adversaries at times, my babysitters, and my first real friends. Nanny and her siblings raised us that way. They are basically my brothers. They *are* my brothers.

Now, even though Lil' Rall and Rasul have always been part of my life, they weren't born in Plainfield like Garrett and me. However, the story of how Lil' Rall and Rasul got to Plainfield is still one of my favorites to hear told. It involves Aunt Cheryl, a station wagon full of babies ranging from one to three years old, Nanny, and her gun. But before we get there, some background on the four of us boys.

Lil' Rall, the oldest of us, was darker skinned, wore glasses, and dealt with asthma—all the makings of cool nerd appeal. He was much more reserved and levelheaded than the rest of the boys most of the time. On the other hand, his younger brother, Rasul, was lighter skinned and a little rough around the edges, but in an adventurous type of way. He was a daredevil. Like, the kind of kid who had never Rollerbladed before, yet upon getting his first pair of Rollerblades for Christmas, put them on, skated out of the living room onto the front porch, jumped down a flight of six steps, and made a perfect landing with the family looking on in shock. Both Lil' Rall and Rasul were taller than me, since they are four and five years older than I am. As a kid, I always found it mind-boggling that they could be brothers, so close in age, with two totally different skin complexions. Childhood naïveté wrapped in innocence, if you will. Lil' Rall and Rasul were also both thinner framed and involved in all sorts of sports. They were "boys" in every sense of the word. I was always much closer to Lil' Rall than I was to Rasul, although I truly cared for both of them.

I was next in line. Although my real name is George, growing up I went by my middle name, Matt (as Nanny used to say, "I'm not calling no little baby *George*"). Since I was born right after Rasul, I was the grandchild who took the attention away from him. Then you had my little brother, Garrett, who came three years after and stole the attention from *me*. Meanwhile, Garrett was and still is "the baby," despite the fact that grandchildren were born after him.

The way we were raised back then, as brothers, influenced how connected we are today. When we text each other now, it's always "love you, big bro" or "talk to you soon, little brother." A cousin can be closer than a brother, and even then, we knew calling each other "brother" meant something.

Plainfield is a small city that is literally only six square miles. On a good day you can get from one end of Plainfield to the other end in less than seven minutes. In 1969, Nanny and her husband (my grandfather, who we used to call "Old Daddy") moved their children from Jersey City to Plainfield. This included Lil' Rall and Rasul's father, Uncle Rall.

Back in the late '70s and early '80s, Uncle Rall, nicknamed by me as just "Uncle," was a rapper, a barber, a drug dealer, and sometimes a drug user. And, according to his stories, he was damn good at whatever profession he was in at the moment. Having grown up in Plainfield, he loved the streets and the streets loved him. He lived a fast life with his then-girlfriend Cynthia. They would eventually get married in 1979 and Cynthia gave birth to Lil' Rall in January 1980. In June 1981, she would give birth to Rasul.

In their early years, Lil' Rall and Rasul lived with their parents in a housing project in Jersey City known as Curries Woods. The projects were low-income housing set up under the guise of "helping" Black and brown folks have their own spaces. In reality, they served as a means to keep us out of "white" neighborhoods, while keeping economic and social systems of oppression in place to further stifle our communities.

Nanny always hated the fact that her grandkids were being raised in and by the projects. Not only were Lil' Rall and Rasul growing up around the selling of drugs, but their parents were using, too. She feared who they might become if they continued living in an environment with two parents who simply weren't equipped at the time to properly care for them. So, she was going to do everything in her power to get them out.

During this time, Nanny ran Weezie's (a nickname for Louise) Wee People Nursery School in the basement of her home. She babysat her grandkids, the children of her children's friends, and other kids from across the city of Plainfield. My mom's best friend, who we refer to as Aunt Cheryl, worked as her assistant. Aunt Cheryl wasn't my aunt by blood, but for most Black folks, family is everything, and we honored her with this title as a sign of respect.

One afternoon at Weezie's Wee People, Nanny was on the phone with Uncle Rall, and their conversation went a little bit to the left. They were discussing Nanny's request for more regular visitation and she expressed her disapproval with my uncle and aunt for running in the streets with the boys. In the background, you could hear Aunt Cynthia calling Nanny all types of "bitch." Nanny didn't take too kindly to my aunt calling her names and she intended to do something about it—*immediately*.

Nanny hung up the phone, and that is where this story really takes flight.

"*Cheryl*," Nanny said. "*Get the kids and put them in the station wagon. We are going to Jersey City!*"

Aunt Cheryl started walking everyone to the station wagon, one by one, as Nanny put on her coat and got ready to handle her business. At the time, there were seven kids in the daycare, including me and Aunt Cheryl's son, Bernard, with none of us big enough to use a regular seat belt. Once they loaded us into the car, Nanny sent Aunt Cheryl into the house to get some towels. She and Aunt Cheryl rolled up the towels, tied them together, stretched them across our laps, and then buckled the towels down so that all of us were secure. Once we were strapped in, Nanny and Aunt Cheryl pulled off, and we were on an adventure to Jersey City.

The ride to Jersey City from Plainfield is thirty-five

to forty minutes on a good day, and that day was a good day. Nanny pulled into the Curries Woods projects, by the building that my uncle and aunt lived in with Lil' Rall and Rasul. This was the mid- to late '80s, so there were no cell phones to call upstairs. Instead, she yelled, asking if anyone knew Rall Elder and, if they did, to tell him that his mother was outside.

Now, from what Uncle says, he heard a knock at his door and opened it to a guy saying, "Man, your mother's downstairs in the lot with a car full of kids. I think you better go talk to her." My uncle knew what was coming, so he told Cynthia to stay in the house, hoping he could calm Nanny down enough to make her go back home. Uncle came outside and down the steps to see my grandmother standing next to the car with a long coat on.

"Mommy," he said, "there is *no* need to do this."

"Naw, she called me a bitch," Nanny responded. "Tell her to come out here and say that to my face."

As my uncle pleaded with Nanny to take the kids and go back home, Aunt Cynthia came running down the steps toward the car. She began calling Nanny every type of b-word you could think of: a "fat b———," an "ugly b———," a dirty b———," and everything under the sun except a child of God. Uncle then recalls what I can only describe as a scene out of *The Matrix*. It all happened in slow motion. My grandmother reached one arm in her coat and, as he described it, pulled out the longest-barreled gun he had ever seen. Everyone in the projects got quiet.

Aunt Cynthia's eyes got as big as quarters before she yelled one final "bitch" and began running for the safety of her apartment. Unfortunately for her, Nanny was just a tad quicker that day and had Cynthia in her sights. By the time Cynthia reached the steps, Nanny caught up and knocked her to the ground with one swing. She hit my aunt twice more with a closed fist. Then she looked at her rings and said, "Awwww, you done got blood in my diamonds," before one final hit. She left Cynthia knocked out, walked back past my uncle, and proceeded to the car like nothing ever happened.

This was always one of my favorite stories to hear because, as beautiful and godly as I remember my grandmother, she was not one to be played with at all. You weren't going to disrespect her and think that it was going to end with her words. "You gotta bring ass to get ass," she would say, and she always brought it.

That Nannyism was the equivalent of a warning shot being fired in the air, letting a person know things could go from verbal to physical really quick if the tone didn't change. It was the threat that wasn't idle, the reminder that the bite better be worse than the bark if you brought that noise in her direction.

When I was younger, I would wonder, *What the hell does that even mean?* As I got older, though, that saying made so much more sense. The closest comparisons to that Nannyism would be "don't start no shit won't be no shit" or "it's on sight." If you talk about what you are going to do to me, then you better be willing to show yourself or bring yourself to actually do it. On another level, it's understanding that you can't get something you never show up for. You can't talk about a thing that you aren't willing to act on. How many times have you said to yourself, "I hope that things improve" without ever doing the work to make it happen? Do you continue hoping for someone else to create the change you want or do you show up for yourself? Do you "bring ya ass" to the situation to get the outcome you desire? Nanny didn't hope that Lil' Rall's and Rasul's lives improved. She took action.

Violence might not be the right way to handle situations. But, being the old-school southern Black woman that she was, as Miss Sofia from *The Color Purple* would say, all her life she had to fight. That meant fighting in person, as well as fighting in a courtroom several months after the Curries Woods incident for full custody over Lil' Rall and Rasul. She knew that she had to get her grandkids out of that life before they, like their parents, became trapped in it, too.

Lil' Rall and Rasul eventually ended up in Plainfield, living with Nanny, Aunt Munch, and my uncle Kevin in what everyone till this day calls "the Big Yellow House." To four little Black boys, the Big Yellow House was a palace and Nanny was the queen. It was the house that had space for every major holiday, birthday, and impromptu family visit. Although Garrett and I didn't reside there, we spent most of our days and weekends at the Big Yellow House because our parents worked long hours and we attended the same school around the corner.

The house had two floors plus a half-finished basement, as well as a medium-sized front yard, where we would play from time to time. A concrete walkway led to the front steps and a small porch landing. Once you entered, the house expanded in every which way. There was a small foyer area with a shelf that held some of Nanny's favorite vases. To the right was the staircase and to the left was a large living room with a couch, a large TV, and a fireplace. Beyond the living room was a den area with an Oriental rug, a piano, and a couch. The first floor also had a dining room, a kitchen, and a sun porch. Upstairs was the bathroom and three bedrooms—Nanny's room, Lil' Rall and Rasul's room, and an extra room, which housed whoever was living in the house at the moment. Lastly, there was a mostly paved backyard and a garage, as well as an empty expanse of grass big enough for its own house. We buried a lot of toy soldiers back there (they're probably there to this day).

In addition to Nanny, the occupants of the palace included Aunt Munch, Lil' Rall, Rasul, and Uncle Kevin (Nanny's nephew, who she adopted when he was eleven years old). Uncle Kevin called her Mommy like the rest of her kids and was raised as their brother, much like Nanny was raising the four of us, her grandkids.

Uncle Kevin was in his late twenties when he lived

with Nanny and became our main babysitter when she had to work. He was dark skinned, bald, and had a knot on the front of his head from a fight years before that we used to make fun of. Uncle Kevin was a constant in our life. He also had a son, Lil' Kevin, who was five years older than me. Lil' Kevin stayed with his mother in Jersey City, though. Uncle Kevin was pretty absent in his life, but not Nanny.

Lil' Kevin would visit several times a year, especially during holidays. He was tall with a dark brown complexion, a medium build, and, age-wise, fell right between Lil' Rall and Rasul. He was always funny and sweet, and every time he came over, he would tell stories about his adventures growing up in Jersey City. Kevin's mother took really good care of him, but if Nanny had it her way, she would have moved Lil' Kevin in, too. Eventually he made his way to Plainfield to stay, but that's much later on in this saga.

As for Lil' Rall and Rasul, Nanny became their primary caregiver and enrolled them in Frederick W. Cook Elementary School, around the corner from the Big Yellow House, in the hope that one day their mother and father would get their act together and be able to take care of them again. In the meantime, Nanny took *care* of them. The term "dressed to the nines" is an understatement about my cousins. They always had the nicest coats, the most expensive sneakers, and the newest video game system. Nanny and her daughters—Aunt Sarah, Aunt Munch, and my mother, Aunt Kaye—spared no expenses on them, and neither did their father, who was still involved in their lives physically and monetarily. A lot of it was an overcompensation for the love they may have been missing out on from their parents. All four of them filled the mother void extremely well.

Lil' Rall and Rasul had a lot of their father's spirit in them. They could rap like their father—with Rasul being the better of the two, in my opinion—and both of them could dance. They were doing on VHS what everyone does now on TikTok and Snapchat. There was a lot of Black joy in our home, but as brothers do, we had our rough spots. Sometimes, Lil' Rall and Rasul would make me and Garrett put on boxing gloves and fight each other—more often for fun, but sometimes to settle disagreements. From time to time, I would get into fights with Rasul, who would always win, being four years my senior. Rasul would fight Lil' Rall for defending me, and they would beat each other up. But in the end, it was always about us and Nanny. Sometimes I think that she enjoyed our chaotic company as much as we enjoyed her being our grandmother. She was like the fifth boy in the crew many times.

As we got older, she would always tell us, "I love all my grandchildren. But I had to love each of you differently because you each needed me for different reasons." However, she still had her favorites, and back then, the breakdown was clear. Lil' Rall was reserved and chill, but he had a special bond with Nanny since he was the first grandchild. Rasul was the adventurous one who wanted to be seen and heard, and Nanny did everything to fill the void left by his mother. I was the loner-geeky-effeminate kid who needed a friend, and she was always there to step in. I would rather read a book than ride a bike, and I loved getting good grades. And Garrett—he was her baby and everyone else's baby, too. Even as a kid, he was strong willed and determined. To the baby went the spoils—and to Garrett went the crown of being her favorite.

We were four little Black boys full of adventure and wonderment. Nanny raised us to know that we could have anything in the world, but family came first. We laughed, we cried, we fussed, fought, lied, and sometimes we got our asses beat. Through it all, we became brothers—brothers raised by our grandmother, who worked hard to ensure we would have a better life. We were Nanny's and she was ours.

Her boys.

Never broken.

2

Saturdaze

Nannyism: "Always put on new underwear,
even if you ain't wash ya ass. You never
know where you'll end up."

Friday nights in the Big Yellow House were never early
nights. My little brother, Garrett, and I went to Nanny's house every day after school, but we knew that
our weekends belonged to her, too. My dad, Gregory,
was a narcotics officer, so he worked really long shifts,
which sometimes included the weekends. He also had
an ingrained patriarchal "king of the castle" mentality,

which meant he had no desire to babysit his own kids during free time. My mother wasn't the stay-at-home type, either. She was always a very independent woman, even within her marriage. She worked five days a week at the police department as the head of the secretaries and also had her own hair salon called Mrs. Kaye's Boutique, where she would spend many nights and most weekends. Suffice it to say, even in a two-parent home, it sometimes takes a village to raise the children. So, when we got to Nanny's house on Friday after school, we already knew the game plan for the weekend. After she got off work, my mom would come by to drop off our clothes and whatever else we needed to get through until Sunday.

I have very fond memories of the weekends Garrett and I spent at the Big Yellow House. Even if we never left the house and played video games all day and night, it was fun for us to be around our cool, big cousins. Even from a very young age, we admired them a lot. I think part of it was that they never seemed annoyed about bringing us along or looking after us.

In addition to running her nursery during the week, Nanny did licensed professional nurse work on the weekends for an older white couple that lived in Madison, New Jersey, about an hour from Plainfield. Therefore, Saturdays were still working days for her. She was a woman of many hustles, as she used to say. Although Uncle Kevin was around (usually sleeping in the basement), she would still leave Lil' Rall in charge of managing the duties she expected us to complete before she got back. Rasul hated that she put Lil' Rall in charge of all of us. Since they were so close in age, he felt he was old enough to handle his own life, or at least old enough to be free from Lil' Rall's rule.

We all used to joke that letting Rasul be the leader could have ended with the house catching on fire. For Rasul, life was a big adventure, full of fun and flare. He knew how to enjoy himself and entertain everyone. But Lil' Rall was more practical and reserved, which meant it was easier to trust him. If he took risks, they were calculated. We didn't want to get in trouble, so we made sure we listened to him. In all honesty, though, I'm sure Rasul would've done fine being in charge from time to time.

Now, Nanny was big on cleanliness—both of body and home. We loved spending time outdoors but when we came in the house, she would be quick to say, "Y'all smell like outside"—and, yes, "outside" has a smell to it. So, making sure we were fresh in the mornings and throughout the day was important to her. Gender roles be damned—no day got started before we took care of our personal hygiene, and eventually cleaned up the rest of the house.

Item 1: Baths

Getting four boys to wake up *and* wash up was no easy task. Even as effeminate as I was, I was a "boy" type of boy whenever I was around Lil' Rall and Rasul— playing in the mud, climbing up trees, running, getting sweaty, jumping in puddles, fighting, all of it. But every Saturday, we all had to take our baths in fifteen-minute intervals so that we were ready by nine AM to get to the next set of tasks.

We went based on age, so Garrett went first. Lil' Rall would help him in the bathroom since he was still young enough to need supervision. Garrett's nickname at the time was "Tuffy," because he was so matter-of-fact and strong willed as a little kid. He often wanted to prove he was "big enough" to wash on his own and sometimes made Lil' Rall stand outside with the door cracked. But Garrett could also be mischievous, so Lil' Rall knew better than to stray too far when it was his turn.

Next up was me. I was allowed to take a bath by myself, though Lil' Rall would help me run the water and make sure I got the temperature right so I wouldn't burn myself. He would then bring my towel and washcloth and say, "You got fifteen minutes."

Even today, the smell of Dove soap always triggers my earliest memories: the white bar of soap, the white porcelain tub, the white-tiled floor, with the light beaming through the window. The bath on Saturday mornings was truly fifteen minutes of peace when my imagination could roam free. While getting all wrinkly, I'd think about what the day would entail and what adventures my cousins and I would go on, until that knock came from Lil' Rall, saying, "It's time to get out, Matt."

One time in the bath, I was doing something I had no business doing. There was this white bar on the wall for hanging washcloths. I, for some reason, thought this bar was made of steel or titanium, and when I tried to hang from it, I quickly learned that it was not. The bar broke in two and I fell in the tub. I just knew Nanny was going to take a switch to my ass that day.

I remember Lil' Rall asking me what happened, and I couldn't even come up with a lie fast enough. He told me to get dressed and that he would handle it. When Nanny got home, Lil' Rall didn't snitch or say I was playing around. Instead, he told her that when I tried to get out of the tub, I slipped and grabbed the bar to catch myself. She looked at us and knew we were lying, but she let it slide that time. I rarely got into trouble, and Lil' Rall helped me keep things that way. He took his role as our guide and protector very seriously and hated seeing any of us get in trouble if he could prevent it.

When I think back, Lil' Rall was very mature for such a young kid. His early years were chaotic, and he probably saw a lot that a kid shouldn't see before the age of seven, but it all made him independent. Still, I wonder which parts of Lil' Rall's childhood are missing because he was responsible for others as early as nine years old. How much of his childhood consisted of him trying to be a big brother to Rasul, trying to protect him when everything around them seemed so messy?

I don't think any harm was intentional. Putting the oldest in charge was simply a tradition passed down from one generation to another in our family. Much like Lil' Rall, my mother was the oldest of her siblings and had the most responsibility. Sometimes she would just allow Uncle Rall to do whatever he wanted because he wasn't trying to listen, but at the end of the day, she was still the one in charge. And during my childhood, Rasul was much like his father, always wanting to be in control. Although it was a hard job, Lil' Rall took pride in being the oldest and knowing he was doing his part to make sure Garrett and I (and even Rasul, when he would listen!) were well-rounded individuals.

After my Saturday bath, I'd dry off and put my underwear on in the bathroom, as well as my tank top. Nanny always believed that little boys should wear undershirts. *"What happens if they get the top shirt dirty or get a stain on it and they ain't got no undershirt?"* As we grew into adults, that phrase transformed into "Always put on clean underwear, even if you ain't washed yo ass." Not to be nasty or distasteful, but I can't tell you how many times in my life I still put on clean under-garments, even if I'm unable to get a full wash or shower in. I'm literally laughing out loud as I write this, thinking about the hypothetical story Nanny used to tell to clown us about what could happen if you weren't wearing clean undergarments:

"Now, what happens if in the middle of the night you get sick and gotta call the ambulance? And then the ambulance comes and takes you to the hospital? Then you get to the hospital and they gotta take your underclothes off and they dirty? Do you want the doctors and nurses who supposed to be saving your life talking about how dirty your underwear was?"

Now, mind you, clean underwear wouldn't change the fact that your body was dirty and might have scents and smells unbecoming to the nose—although you couldn't tell Nanny that. But I think, as real as this was, it was also a larger metaphor for how you should look your most presentable and be prepared for anything. I'm almost certain that, even as adults, all four of us wear either a T-shirt or a tank top underneath our clothes. It is an instinct that is embedded in us, so much so that I feel uncomfortable when I'm not wearing one or forget to pack one. Those lessons we learned as little boys never went away. The power of the Black proverb, I reckon.

Anyhoo, after I partially dressed in the bathroom, I'd head to Lil' Rall and Rasul's room, where Lil' Rall had already laid out my outfit on the bed, and proceed to get dressed. Meanwhile, I'd overhear a normal Saturday-morning argument, which consisted of Rasul reminding Lil' Rall that he was not the boss of him, despite knowing the requests were coming from command central, aka Nanny. And most Saturdays, Rall would just walk off and say, "Do what you want, Rasul!" I honestly think Rasul just wanted everything to be his decision and not something demanded of him, especially by his older brother. Regardless, once everyone was washed and dressed, we moved on to the next step.

Item 2: Chores

Once again, Rall was left with the responsibility of handing out tasks and making sure everything got done. I often wonder if Nanny's religious faith was connected to her strong beliefs in keeping clean and keeping a clean house. The saying goes that "cleanliness is next to godliness," and Nanny made sure that her boys were as close as possible to the Lord's likeness and image. After bath time, Lil' Rall would cut on some music, usually old-school R&B on the radio, and we would all get to cleaning.

Rasul was responsible for sweeping the entire house. Lil' Rall was responsible for mopping after Rasul finished sweeping a room. I was responsible for dusting the wood furniture and Nanny's large purple vases throughout the house, as well as cleaning the crystal dishes. Garrett just helped out by wiping or holding the paper towels for us.

We worked at a moderate pace and it would usually take us two to three hours to get everything done. We didn't really argue much about having chores, unless Rasul got mad because he wanted to mop instead of sweep, or Lil' Rall got bossy with the demands. Also, we knew Nanny was not to be played with. She was the kindest, coolest woman in the world—but she also was an authoritarian. Doing chores was as much a part of our Saturday routine as going outside and riding bikes.

As an adult, I know that cleaning up after oneself is something that *everyone* should do, but *everyone* isn't conditioned that way. To be clearer, boys are not often conditioned this way. Girls get dolls at a very young age to teach them to take care of babies later in life. They get Easy-Bake Ovens and are taught to cook, clean, and take care of a household. Although boys will become the fathers to many of these babies, they are not encouraged to feed and hold a baby from that same age. Instead, boys are pushed to be firefighters or cops or construction workers—some form of a profession that conditions them to be the providers and protectors to women. To take it a step further, boys are often shamed for being interested in things deemed "feminine." A boy "shouldn't" play with dolls and makeup or play games like double Dutch. Double Dutching was something I actually had to stop doing for safety around boys who were calling me a faggot, so I know from experience. Too often, society has ruined Black boys.

I grew up in a household where my father did not pick up after himself. Even to this day when I stay at home with my parents, I find myself picking up after my dad. But he was conditioned by his dad, who had his mom pick up after them their whole lives. She did so well into her seventies until she no longer could. So, it wasn't as if we didn't see how patriarchy operated when it came to men and women, or boys and girls. It's just that our grandmother Nanny had a different agenda and taught us to be well-rounded individuals. She didn't see the responsibility of cleaning up as one based on gender—she just saw it as a practice for every child to learn.

She operated in all spaces like that, though. It's part of the reason that she was adamant that all her kids made it through high school (and some through college), even when their cousins weren't pushed in the same way. She raised all of her children as full individuals who could dream, who could be and do anything they wanted. Everyone could cook. Everyone could clean. Of course, it didn't necessarily prevent her kids from getting involved in drugs or making bad decisions, but she made sure the tools were there, that they had the knowledge, and that they always had a home.

As an adult, I love waking up on a Saturday morning and just cleaning up. I cut on the old-school R&B and think about an easier time, when there were no bills but tons of adventures. Her lessons speak volumes in my mind about preparedness, cleanliness, and always having your space presentable.

The reward for completing our Saturday chores always differed. Sometimes Nanny would make breakfast food for dinner. Or she would get the ingredients for homemade ice cream sandwiches. I would always microwave mine to make the ice cream soft and warm, while Lil' Rall and Rasul called me weird. Garrett just made a mess, and we had to clean up after him.

But then, sometimes we'd get the *big* reward.

"Rall, Rasul, Matt, and Garrett. Put your sneakers on—we are going out!"

The four of us would head out to the car, wondering where she was taking us that day. A restaurant, the mall, a theme park—wherever she wanted to surprise us. From the back seat windows of the station wagon, we would watch the houses become trees, become the sky, wondering where our next adventure with Nanny would take us. We were just four Black boys and their grandmother, making forever memories as the daylight became moonlight glowing on our skin, as radiant as the Black boy joy that lived within.

LIL' RALL TO NANNY

Dear Nanny,

Thank you.

Thank you for taking two boys from the projects and showing them unconditional love. You took the responsibility of raising us when our parents were not mature enough to care for us properly. You showed us what compassion, strength, and determination looked like. Often, when I close my eyes and think back to my earliest memories, I see your face. Christmases, birthdays, and Easters, we never went without.

Believe it or not, I remember going into the courtroom during my parents' custody hearing. I was probably six or seven, and heading into that big building, with all those people, made me anxious. I remember walking in with my dad and the very moment he gave my hand to the bailiff. I remember feeling nervous and the bailiff smiling and speaking, though I can't recall what he said. I remember seeing a man with a big black robe waiting outside of an office. Then I remember seeing you standing next to Aunt Sarah and Aunt Munch, and when you waved at me, I knew that things were going to be okay.

That morning, the judge asked me and my brother who we would rather live with. It was not that direct—the question was, "If all of your toys were with Mom, and Dad was in another place, where do you think you would want to stay?" As any kid would have, I said, "Wherever the toys were." Suffice it to say, the toys wound up at your house and so did my brother and I. We were so fortunate to have such a wonderful upbringing. You refused to let your grandbabies end up in foster care. You made sure that we felt loved.

Though our needs were different, you made time for the both of us—soon to be the four of us, with the addition of Matt and Garrett. And five, when Lil' Kevin would come around. I am not sure how you did it, honestly. You were my team mom when I played baseball, assistant troop leader for my Boy Scout troop, and if there was anything we showed interest in, you were involved in one way or another. Even though Matt and Garrett were my cousins, you told me that you were raising us like brothers because one day we would only have each other.

I took that so seriously. I always wanted to protect them. At times, that weighed heavily on me. I felt like I had so much responsibility and wanted to escape—not because I did not love them or you, but because I just needed my own space. I believe you sensed that, but you always wanted me close to keep me from turning to the streets like my father and uncles.

You and I had a deep connection. I would come home from high school and training after school at the boxing gym, and just lie at the foot of your bed and we would watch *The Golden Girls*. As I got older, that became our bonding time. So, when I decided to leave for the military, I did not want to say anything because I knew it would hurt you. We would no longer have our time together once I left. I waited until the day before I shipped out to tell you. I saw the pain in your face, and it broke me, but I also knew that you prepared me for whatever was thrown my way. Months later, the pride on your face when I graduated from basic training made it worth it. You were so happy and so proud, and that was all I ever wanted. You wanted to celebrate but I just wanted to nap. You just said, "You worked hard, baby. Take a break."

As we grew older, the boys and I separated and became men in our own right. But we made sure we stayed in contact. You never said call them, you would just imply that it needed to be done.

"Have you spoken to Matthew?"

"No, ma'am, I'll call him."

"Garrett is headed to Virginia."

"I'll reach out to make sure he's okay."

"Where is Rasul?"

"Nanny, I don't chase that boy."

"He needs you."

"Yes, ma'am."

You only had to say it and I knew that I needed to check on my boys. I promise to keep up on that.

Even though I am the oldest, you treated me like I was still your baby. Last year, when my family and I moved back to New Jersey, you would call to make sure that I got on the train and wasn't lost in the city.

"Lil' Rall, you all right? Where you at?"

"On the train, Nanny. Headed home from work."

"Well, you be careful."

"Nanny, I'm thirty-eight. I've been traveling by myself since I was seventeen."

"Well, I don't know nothing about that, just be careful."

"Yes, ma'am."

That year back in Jersey, I felt like a teenager again. I loved taking you to movies on a whim, picking you up and driving down to Virginia, treating you to birthday dinners, and sneaking glass-bottle Cokes past Aunt Kay and Aunt Sarah on Sundays. I do not know if it was God or some divine blessing, but it seemed like I was supposed to come home at that time.

Toward the end of my time back, you got sick. It was sudden and felt like a shock wave to us all. Our rock, the one that guided us, was not herself. Matt took the lead, and I cannot express how proud of them I am. You would be so amazed at how they handled the logistics of everything after you left. I want you to know that you left a legacy here. The family is well, and we are staying connected because that is how you raised us. Your boys are tighter than ever. I will make sure to check on my brothers because I need them, too.

I miss you so much.

Love Your First Grand,
Rall Lynwood Elder III

3

They Both Did It

Nannyism: "I'm putting everybody in a paper bag and shaking it up, the one that fall out first I'm whooping they ass."

The Bible says "spare the rod and spoil the child." Whoever wrote that line must've had a grandmother like Nanny. 'Cause in Nanny's house, if you messed up, not only were you going to get the rod to that backside, but you were going to be the one to go fetch it, too. "Spankings" were part of our culture. When Nanny was a child and messed up, she got spanked. Her kids messed up, they got spanked. It was passed down like Grandma Lula Mae's mac-and-cheese recipe.

When I think of the phrase "they used to fight like cats and dogs," I immediately think about what it was like growing up with Lil' Rall and Rasul. I would often be there for their weekly altercations, which were always knock-down, drag-'em-out brawls. Brawls eventually got both of their asses whooped—although, depending on who tells the story, one got more than the other. The two of them loved each other hard, but they also fought hard.

Most weekends we were good. We usually finished all our chores and had our normal boys' days filled with video games and bike rides. However, some of those Saturdays were complete war zones, with Lil' Rall on one side and Rasul on the other. Garrett and I often played the audience or the referee, depending on how bad the situation got.

However, there's one Saturday in particular that I will never forget. I had to have been about seven years old at the time, making Lil' Rall and Rasul around the ages of twelve and eleven, respectively. In my mind, the moment plays out like a scene from a movie. It was one of those experiences that you could never replicate, even if you tried a thousand times. And I think it was just so damn funny to me because, even as a kid, I was tired of Lil' Rall and Rasul's fighting, just like everyone else. I loved my cousins dearly, but sometimes their fighting just didn't make any sense. Although Garrett and I were three years apart, I can probably count on one hand the amount of times we've physically gotten into it, in thirty-plus years of life. Lil' Rall and Rasul could easily get into it five times a week.

That day, they got into one of their normal back-and-forth arguments. Truth be told, I'm not even sure if it was an argument over chores, video games, or Rasul hitting me. But whatever it was, it started out with words and then transformed into a fistfight. Now, be clear, we all *knew* what fights led to: Nanny coming home and somebody getting a spanking. Yet we still played with fire.

I was standing in the front entrance of the house by the stairs. Garrett must've been upstairs, because he wasn't anywhere around the commotion. But Lil' Rall and Rasul stood about ten feet in front of me, arguing at the front entrance of the living room. I remember being frozen and looking at the two of them like, *Are we really doing this AGAIN?* As the fight escalated from verbal to physical, they started throwing punches at each other. Both could fight well, so it wasn't like one was winning and one was losing. It was just mutual combat.

A few days prior, Nanny had purchased a brand-new coffee table. It was a beautiful shade of light brown and sat between her favorite chair and the fireplace. If memory serves me right, it was a circular table. You could tell she spent a lot of money on it because of how polished and clean it looked. And because Nanny was not cheap about anything, everything she purchased for herself cost a pretty penny.

As they threw punches, they moved toward the new coffee table. The fight looked like the Tasmanian Devil when he started spinning and destroying everything in sight. It was just punches and kicks and punches and kicks and cursing. With each blow they were moving ever so close to that table. I just stood there in silence and watched. My teeth were clenching because I already could tell what was about to go down. What seemed to take forever in my mind was probably only ten seconds long, but when that moment finally happened, it *happened*.

In unison, both of them lifted their legs to avoid the table and instead came down right *on* the table. Nanny's brand-new wooden table. With a loud *CRACK*, it was all over. The fight stopped immediately. And there the three of us stood—me by the stairs with my mouth open, Lil' Rall on the left side of the now-broken table, and Rasul to the right of it. I think we were all in a state of shock.

Like in a scene out of a movie, we heard that station wagon door slam. There was literally nothing we could do but face whatever we were going to face. Fifteen seconds passed from the slam of the car door to the sound of her walking up those wooden front-porch steps. The screen door creaked and the main door opened. And then there was Nanny.

Nanny was only five feet three, but at that moment she seemed seven feet tall. There were many other times as boys that we messed up—getting a bad grade on a paper or not doing a chore or task we were asked to do. But this time seemed like the ultimate mess-up, one I had nothing to do with. And I definitely did not want to partake in the ass whooping I knew was coming for the guilty parties.

Nanny just stood there, looking at the two of them and her new table in shambles. "What happened?" she said. Immediately the two of them got to pointing fingers and explaining their side.

"Shut up! Both of you be quiet." They immediately shut up. Nanny then looked at me. "Matt, who did this to the table?"

I looked at Rall. I looked at Rasul. Then I answered as honestly as I could.

"Both of 'em!"

They each looked at me and said, "*Matt!*" To which I said, "They started fighting and they both went through the table."

"Go outside and get me a switch," Nanny said.

Rall and Rasul immediately started crying. At this point, the two of them knew what was coming next: that dreaded walk of shame.

While some folks used belts for a whooping, southern folks used a switch. A switch is a thin, wispy branch from a tree, usually with the leaves removed. Like many other traditions passed down, I'm almost certain that breaking the switch off the tree was something done for generations in our family. When Nanny and her brothers and sisters got together, they would talk about the ass whoopings their parents gave them with the switch. It was like a rite of passage. Sharing family stories around spankings means something, and that something is trauma. It's one that is rarely named because it's considered a part of the culture, but even culture can be traumatic. And sometimes it needs to be changed.

That walk to find a switch was always the worst part, as you just knew that you were about to face the worst of it. Also, you had to make sure you got the right-sized branch, or you would get in even more trouble for playing around with your impending beating. Choosing the item that you were about to be punished with was a trauma in and of itself, followed by the trauma of the actual beating.

Rall went outside and found a tree in the backyard and broke a small, thin branch off it. Crying, he came back in with the switch and handed it to Nanny. Rasul stood off to the side as Nanny grabbed Lil' Rall by one arm and began swatting him across his backside. The switch would cut through the air and make a *whisk* noise before making impact. There's a saying in our community: "I'm a beat you until I get tired." You usually got eight to ten swats before you started wriggling your body, and then the hits would stop. She then did the same thing to Rasul—another eight to ten swats before letting him go.

"Now go upstairs to your room!" Nanny said before sending them away.

Both of them, now fully sobbing, went upstairs to the bedroom. I followed behind them. That day was one of the quietest times I ever remember having in one another's presence. Garrett—the always-inquisitive-never-afraid-to-make-a-statement child—of course, asked loudly, "What happened to y'all? What happened to y'all?" Lil' Rall responded, "Be quiet, Garrett." We all just sat on the edge of the bed. Four little Black and brown-complexioned boys on brown sheets with sad faces.

"Why you have to say it was both of us, Matt?" said Lil' Rall.

"Because it was," I said. "Y'all *both* did it."

And there we sat. What seemed like an eternity was really only ten to fifteen minutes, but it gave us all enough time to decompress together. We had all been on that walk before to the tree to get a switch. And at that moment, the four of us stuck together, even if we all hadn't gotten whooped. If one of us got in trouble, we all felt like we got in trouble. We never wanted to do anything that couldn't include all of us. Even through all of our bickering and fighting, it was all for one and one for all.

Despite the good times we had, I know we hold on to the trauma of spankings. I can actually count on one hand all the whoopings I received. One time I snuck into the kitchen and was lighting napkins on fire. I got caught by Uncle, and that was the only time he whooped me. Once, when I was thirteen, I was whooped by Dad for getting into a fight with Garrett and choking him. And I was whooped once by Nanny, but I don't recall what it was for.

Garrett? The baby of the crew? Although he was Nanny's favorite, Garrett was always getting into something. One time, when he was about eight or nine, he changed an F on his report card to an A. When he came home from school, the first person to get to him was Nanny. She gave him that whooping that day. A few minutes later, Garrett came back into the room with a jump and said he was going to hang himself. Nanny whooped him again for being so "dramatic."

My oh my, how times have changed—and with good reason. There is a belief that brutality works as a way toward curbing poor behaviors. Many Black kids share the same type of stories about getting whoopings. As I stated earlier, it was a generational practice passed down, like a recipe or a family heirloom. The technical term for it is "corporal punishment," and for many of us that have been through it, it is a trauma. Whooping introduces power dynamics through violence, and furthermore, there is no concrete way to measure where a whooping ends and where chargeable violence and abuse begin. One must admit that *all* of it is violence under the guise that one is considered "acceptable," and the other isn't.

Violence and punishment have long been the system's answers to everything. Going back to the trans-atlantic slave trade, Black Americans historically were subjected to extreme violence, including whippings, among other abuses, at the hands of the then-dominant white community. We were indoctrinated in violence, conditioned through and by violence, and colonized to adopt it as our own.

In a broader sense today, we live in a society where punishment is the primary form of "justice" for bad choices. Rather than break down right from wrong, we teach children that there is a violent consequence for wrong actions. But, when do we ever teach children *why* an action was wrong? Or what the better solution would be the next time? Do we just keep beating them with the hope one day "it"—a sense of right and wrong—will magically click?

As young Black boys, we were groomed to fight and use violence as a tool of power and as an entry point to masculinity. There isn't a doubt in my mind that the violence we saw and experienced contributed to the violence we may have enacted. When a parent felt wronged by a partner, we witnessed verbal and, at times, physical abuse. When a parent felt upset or wronged by a child, we experienced abuse. When we felt wronged or harmed by one another, we committed violence upon each other. It's a cycle of abuse that needs to end.

Earlier, I said that Lil' Rall and Rasul's fight could easily have started in defense of me. As an adult, I can process the issues Rasul was dealing with as a child. He was constantly facing Lil' Rall, the older, somewhat bigger, somewhat stronger brother that always seemed in control, that always seemed to have power, that was always fighting him. In many ways, Rasul needed to feel that same power and would take it all out on me, on my face and on my body. Boys just being boys, as many would say. But the trauma of those fights with Rasul, who was four years older than me, never left. I held on to it because I never won against him. The one time I finally swung back, I was eleven or twelve and we were nearly the same height and weight. As usual, he was messing with me, so I punched him in his face. Rasul grabbed me by both shoulders.

"Don't ever hit me again like that, Matt!" he yelled before he walked off.

Even now, I remember the power I felt in hitting him and knowing I hurt him the same way he hurt me. We never fought again and, honestly, I can't think of a time ever as young adults or adults that we felt the need to get physical with one another—but I didn't immediately let go of the pain and frustration. Years later, at age eighteen, when I moved to college, I hung out with Rasul and finally got it all out. I told him that he was very mean and hurtful to me as a child and that I never forgot it. I told him that it took a long time to forgive him for the fighting, but that I still loved him. He received it. Apologized. Told his side of things—which at the time I felt was still centering him—but I understood. I'm fortunate that the two of us have a great relationship now, but that took work and face-to-face talks as adults to peace it up. In many ways, the four of us are still unpacking, healing.

Beating a child as a form of discipline today will likely end with you in jail or a child-protection case. It is not taken lightly or accepted by most standards on discipline. Kids carry trauma, and there is nothing about a whooping that doesn't instill a harmful behavior. You will hear many say that beatings helped or changed their lives, and one can't deny someone else's truth. I could easily say we got beatings and we turned out "okay," but there was a lot that was *not* "okay" before the four of us got to where we are now. We have many family members who went through that same version of discipline who still ain't "okay" and will likely never be "okay." Some ways about us just shouldn't be passed down. Some things just have to be stopped.

Eventually Rall, Rasul, Garrett, and I went back downstairs to see if Nanny had cooled off. When we finally stood in front of her, we all apologized. All four of us. All for one and one for all. Nanny could get angry with the best of them, but she always said, "You can't get to heaven with a grudge on your heart." So, even in the moments when we pissed her off the most, the love soon returned. I guess in many ways the love never left. The "beating" for all intents and purposes came from a place of love. *I'm harming you because I love you and I want you to learn pain as a consequence of messing up.* Still, I can't help but wonder—what if love was the consequence of messing up? Not violence, but talking? Accountability? Processing?

The problem lies in the fact that violence was ever labeled as a form of love to begin with. I have no ill will toward Nanny for any beating I ever received, but I also know that all four of us are working through that trauma differently. It's more than a means to heal ourselves. It's a chance to change the trajectory of how our family and our community rights a wrong, absent the violence and abuse we have internalized from white supremacy and the systems above us. I look back on those moments and I see lessons learned and moments that we all can grow from.

Tough love never needs violence. Love never needs abuse.

4

You'll Shoot Your Eye Out

Nannyism: "I'll be on your ass like forty
going North."

Some of the best stories are those that I don't fully remember. Stories where I don't remember how we traveled to get to a place. Stories where I can't recall the details of the house or hotel room where we stayed. Stories where I don't remember the full scope of the day or even who might have been there. But sometimes certain moments and conversations stay with me forever.

One specific moment, during the summer of 1991,

certainly sticks out because of how it made me feel. It's a memory with Rall, Rasul, Garrett, and some of our other cousins on the Elder side of the family. It was a defining day in my life, when I proved I was just as adult as my older cousins.

That summer, we went to the country for a family reunion cookout. The whole clan traveled to Mecklenburg and Lunenburg Counties in Virginia, where the Elder side of our family started. The rumor was always that we Elders had Irish in our blood. There was also a rumor that we had Indigenous people in our family. As an adult, I actually took the time to research this, just to see if I could trace our lineage back. Elder *is* an Irish surname, and I was able to trace my family to the 1860 census, the first time anyone Black with the last name Elder showed up in those counties. In the prior census I found, from 1830, the only Elders listed were white Irish. Suffice it to say, it is very likely that the white Elders owned enslaved Africans, who they subsequently had nonconsensual sex with (rape), birthing the start of the Elder side of my family. For Christmas of 2018, Aunt Munch and I took the 23andMe test to see which family story about our beginnings was true. It came back for both of us that we had 0 percent Indigenous DNA matches. However, a small percentage of Irish showed up, confirming what we had long thought. Irish was somewhere in our lineage, and it didn't get there willingly.

Anyway, this memory of the family reunion gets a little fuzzy because I was only six at the time, but I can piece most of it together. That summer day, we were out in the country by one of our family's houses. That whole weekend I had been able to hang with everyone, so I automatically assumed that this would be no different—except it was. My uncle Rall, my mother, and a few of the other adults were discussing going down the hill to shoot this gun and taking some of the cousins to experience it. I probably had no business standing there, listening to grown folks' business. But, hearing what they were saying, I was so intrigued.

As everyone started down the hill, including Rall and Rasul, I was told that I was too young to join. I pleaded with everyone for the chance to come, but they didn't want to risk it.

"Next time, Matt," my mother told me. She knew I was disappointed, but she also was looking out for my safety.

I honestly had no business even thinking about shooting a real gun, but, let's face it, it seemed like a cool thing to do. My father was a police officer, so I had seen guns before. Furthermore, we played with cap guns, Nerf guns, and toy guns all the time. Why play with those guns if it wasn't to prepare me for the big moment? Mind you, these were the thoughts of a six-year-old who wasn't correlating the danger of a real weapon with being shot with Nerf darts by Rall and Rasul.

There they all went, walking down the hill, and there I sat, upset. From my spot at the top I could hear every shot. Each of the cousins between the ages of ten and sixteen took a turn. It was one of those once-in-a-lifetime experiences as a kid that you are sworn not to talk about outside the family. *Don't go running your mouth to friends and teachers.* We were still Black kids, and there was no need to give anyone the inference that we had access to a gun, let alone ever used one.

In the distance, I could see the family walking back. As they came closer, I knew I had one more chance. My elated cousins all walked past as I waited for Uncle to come up the hill. I immediately ran over to him and decided to "shoot my shot," pun intended.

Quick backstory. When Rall and Rasul first moved to Plainfield, I was a little boy no more than two years old. My early memories of their father, my uncle Rall, start around the time I was age four or five. Because I didn't know who he was when he used to visit, I would see him and simply say, "Yo!" One day he was in the living room and said, "Hey, Matt!" and I responded, "Yo!" He pulled me to the side and said, "Matt, don't call me 'Yo,' I'm your uncle. Call me Uncle." From that day, his name to all the nieces and nephews became simply "Uncle." So, anytime I refer to "Uncle" with no name after it, it is Uncle Rall, my mother's brother. My second father.

That day on the hill, I looked right up at him and said, "I didn't get to shoot the gun, Uncle." Not knowing what to say, Uncle looked over to my mother, hoping she could get us all out of this situation. But before she could say anything, I looked at her and said, "Mommy, tell Uncle that I didn't get to shoot the gun." Now they *both* were stuck, 'cause I was "on they asses like forty going North," as Nanny used to say. Meaning, I had all the spirit and enthusiasm in the world— I was determined to shoot that gun, and nothing was going to stop me. My mother and uncle had a decision to make. Break a child's heart into pieces or go against everything they thought was right and let me shoot that gun?

My uncle then looked over at Solidene, one of the cousins on the Elder side of the family. As far as the name goes, it could be pronounced "Soul-li-dean" or "Sal-li-dean" or "Soul-le-dune," depending on how drunk you were when saying it. He was in his early thirties and darker skinned, with a stocky build. My most vivid memory with him was a trip to the supermarket with another family member. After waiting about thirty minutes in the car, I walked in to find him. And find him, I did...with his shorts and underwear around his ankles, drunk, sleeping on the toilet. It was a reminder never to drink corn liquor in the heat.

"Dene," Uncle said, "we gonna have to let this little nigga shoot the gun."

Solidene looked at him and said, "A-ite, let's do it."

"Come on, Matt," my mother said as she stood, "let's go shoot the gun."

The four of us went walking down that dirt hill to the spot where everyone had been shooting. I was excitedly nervous. I had been playing with toy guns for as long as I could remember, which at the age of six or seven doesn't mean many years of thoughts. However, I knew that the joy from playing with toy guns with my cousins didn't match the delight I was feeling. I'm sure my guardians walking me down felt quite differently, though. Nervous. Worried. Scared was probably closest to what they felt. We finally reached the bottom of the hill.

"Come on, Matt," said Uncle.

I walked over to him and he stood behind me. He positioned my hands on the weapon to fire at a can that sat on a wooden fence post about 100 feet away. He put my tiny right hand over the butt of the gun and told me to put my index finger over the trigger.

I felt strong at that moment. I felt tough at that moment. For a kid that felt like he wasn't like the other boys in the family, this showed I was still one of them. In many ways, I was usually the "soft" cousin: emotional, effeminate, but never shunned. I was different and, at this moment, I finally got to be like everyone else.

"All right, Matt, you ready to pull the trigger?"

Uncle asked. "Make sure you hold on tight, or it's gonna break your wrist."

"Okay, Uncle." I took a deep breath and then squeezed down.

BANG!

My little body jolted back. I could feel my arm vibrating from the power of the gun. I shot it. I didn't care that I didn't hit the can or couldn't even see where the bullet landed. I had really shot my first gun. I looked back at Uncle and smiled. Uncle was happy. My mom was glad it was over.

Uncle took the gun from me and then handed it over to Cousin Solidene before we walked back up the hill toward the house. As we made our way, I had my chest poked out and my head held high. Marching almost with my arms pumping in the wind. My uncle always says that I was walking back "like I had conquered the world." He still references Puss in Boots, the boisterous cat from the Shrek movies, walking into the room like he owned it.

Despite my pride that day, it's important to recognize that the images we see on television and in the media about white boys and guns are much different from those of Black boys. Many white boys from a very young age are taught to shoot, hunt, and believe that guns are their birthright, while Black boys like us had to do it in secrecy. It can't be lost on us that in this country, a Black boy with a gun is equal to his death. A Black boy with a *toy* gun is equal to his death. White boys get hunting guns for Christmas. Black boys like us resorted to traveling to a different state, in the country-side, where no one could see us have that "experience." White boys are led down paths of gun ownership, with law and order and weapons as a means to an end. Black boys are sat down for the "talk." Not the talk about the birds and the bees and sex, even though many of us get that talk, too. There is another talk that occurs in Black households—one that has been given for gener-ations with haunting reminders of just how disposable our lives can be to others, even if all instructions are followed. The talk about how to survive police officers. The talk about how to survive overt racism while also having the ability to navigate covert racism. The talk about how you can do everything right and still end up wronged in a society that is anti-Black.

If you get pulled over, put both hands on the steering wheel and wait for the cop to come to the car. Don't reach for anything unless you are either told to or ask for permission to reach for it. State out loud what you are reaching for. Try not to get smart with the officer. Less talking is better.

Generations ago, this talk used to sound like *Don't look a white person in the eyes and stare, it's a sign of disrespect. Don't whistle at a white woman. When you see a white person walking and you are in their path, move out of the way.*

Do everything Master says. Don't resist.

Do everything the officer says. Don't resist.

There have been centuries of preparing Black boys for leaving the house, with the simple fact of Black maleness being a threat. It's why, even though Garrett and I had dozens of toy guns, we were not allowed to go outside with them. We could do whatever we wanted with them indoors, but we knew we were in trouble if we stepped out of the house with them. Furthermore, we were told explicitly why. "A cop could mistake it for a real gun and shoot you."

Guns and Black boys don't mix, like water and oil. And although there is Black gun ownership in this country, we have also seen the death of Black people at the hands of police for legally carrying their weapons—juxtaposed against images of white militias proudly walking and "bearing arms" in front of police officers who never seem to be afraid of their skin folks proudly carrying.

This memory of shooting my first gun stands out not just because of the power I or any of my cousins felt at that moment, but also because of how I feel today, knowing that the moment was never meant to be. It was a secret to keep among ourselves. I've never shot a gun since that day, although Garrett, Rall, and Rasul most certainly have. But I'll always have the memory of my first and only time shooting, the constant reminder why many never will have that experience, and the sobering fact that for some it could be their last.

5

Barbershop Talk

Nannyism: "It's a sad rabbit that only got one hole."

The first haircut. It's a rite of passage that most Black boys will go through, another one of those unofficial traditions in our community.

I don't recall my first haircut. To be fair, I don't think any of us remembers when we got our first haircut. However, I've watched enough kids get that first big chop to know that it is never an easy situation. The sound of those clippers evokes a fear never felt before.

I've watched kids jump out the chair and take off running. Kids move their head so much that their parents have to hold it in place while they scream and cry. That first haircut is never the beautiful moment that parents want it to be.

When I was growing up in Plainfield, there was never a time when my family wasn't operating a barbershop or beauty salon. Nanny always taught us it was important to have multiple ways to make money. *It's a sad rabbit that only got one hole*—meaning, that rabbit is easily trapped. What happens if the hole closes up or is filled in? What happens if the hunter comes and you've only got one move to make? Essentially, she meant "don't put all your eggs in one basket." Always have options and utilize all your talents to make your money.

My mother started a hair salon when we were really young—Mrs. Kaye's Boutique, located on South Avenue in Plainfield, New Jersey. It was the ultimate family business. The salon was spacious, with three separate sections. It was definitely a whole grooming situation happening in the early '90s, very comparable to the services you see today from "spas" and exclusive places. In the first section, you had the hairstylists. My mother,

Uncle, and some of her other friends—Mrs. Tina, Ms. Lorraine, Lee May, Flintstone—made up the team. Yes, Uncle could do hair. And I mean he could *do* hair. Truth be told, between his cool looks, charming ways, and ability to do hair, he was easily a magnet for some of the women who came to the salon, including my future aunt Crystal. By this point, Rall and Rasul's mother, Cynthia, was pretty nonexistent. There were visits here and there, but after Nanny took them in, she wasn't really much in their lives. But Aunt Crystal? I will never forget the first time she came into the salon. She used to work at the police department as a secretary, so she knew my mother and started coming in to get her hair done. Her nickname was Honey, and she was always one of the most beautiful women I can remember. She was lighter skinned and reminded me of the singer Faith Evans. Uncle eventually started doing her hair. They started dating, and the rest is history. To this day he still helps her with hair from time to time.

In the middle section of Mrs. Kaye's Boutique were the nail technicians. My mother had several nail techs, including my aunt Sarah, who worked part-time. Finally, there was a third room, which was the boutique that Nanny ran as another of her side hustles. She sold hats, clothes, and jewelry.

One of my favorite moments in the beauty salon was when Rall, Rasul, Garrett, and I would harmonize together. As little boys we all sang in the Mount Zion AME Church choir. You'll hear more about that later on, but suffice it to say, Nanny's boys could carry a tune. We all knew our parts in the song, where to come in high or low under one another. I actually wish we would have kept up with singing. My mother is an amazing vocalist and could have gone professional if she'd wanted to. Plus, our grandfather Old Daddy could sing and play the guitar. It was truly in our blood.

There was a very popular song out by Shai, a male singing group that consisted of four members. Male R&B groups were very big in the '90s. Every one of them had a hit or two. Many of the groups didn't stay popular long, but their music lasted forever. The name of their hit was "If I Ever Fall in Love" and it reached number two on the Billboard Hot 100. The song had so many runs in it, with one really big note at the end.

The four of us boys were in the salon one day and decided we were going to sing this song for the customers.

At the time, Garrett was four, I was seven, Rasul was eleven, and Rall was twelve. Sitting atop stools, Lil' Rall took the lead, Rasul took second lead, and I did the background vocals while Garrett sat watching.

Me and Rasul started with the background vocals. "*Dooooooo, da do, do, dooooooo da do, do!*"

Lil' Rall sang the first line: "*The very first time, that I saw your brown eyes, your lips said hello and I said hi . . .*"

The barbershop–beauty shop, our own little captive audience, was loving every moment of it. We finally got to the end of the song, where Rasul came in to take the lead.

"*My frieeeeeeeeeeeeeeeeeeeeeeeeennnnnnnddddddd,*" Rasul sang over and over while we provided back up. Each time he sang the line, he went an octave higher. When he got to the fourth "my friend," that was where he had to hit the high note—think of the whistle note Mariah Carey uses in many of her songs. Mind you, we had practiced together but we weren't sure of Rasul's range until he got to that note. Rasul leaned back and inhaled. He then let it out:

"*my FRIIIIIIEEEEEEENNNNNNDDDDDDDDD!*"

Everyone in the salon started clapping and cheering.

"You better sing, Rasul!" someone yelled.

Funny enough, the second time he went for that note to close the song, he hit it, but forgot we were on stools—while leaning back to sing, he fell right off. We all started laughing, but the salon continued clapping for us.

My mother owned the salon during most of our adolescent years, but eventually Uncle decided to branch out on his own and open his own barbershop out of the front of his house on South Avenue in Plainfield. The house was within walking distance of our school, and for a two-year period, Uncle's house became a regular visit for me and Garrett. In addition to going there every day after class, my mom would drop us off at Uncle's new barbershop on Saturday mornings before she headed to the hair salon.

Garrett loved Saturdays at the shop because he loved getting a haircut. Even as a kid, he was very much into looks. He always wanted the newest sneakers and started his Jordan collection at around the age of seven or eight. Although Garrett may have been the baby, he took pride in how he looked, and that included his haircut. He *always* had some design in his head. Whether it was a simple part or a zigzag, he liked to be well groomed and flashy. Garrett today is a direct manifestation of the kid that he was then—very independent and matter-of-fact. If he saw a certain haircut, he would come in there knowing exactly what he wanted. We also used to call Garrett "big head," which I know he hated, so a perfect haircut meant a lot to him (even if it was just a distraction from his big dome).

I'll be honest. At first, I hated going to the barbershop on Saturdays. But that was mainly because the first few weekends she dropped us off for our haircuts, I thought she was coming back soon. However, on those days Uncle would cut hair from eight AM until midnight, and we were *always* the last heads he would cut, unless he had a break between customers. But once I got over the first few visits, the barbershop became fun. Rall and Rasul were well into their teens, which meant they had better things to do than stick with me and Garrett all day. They were around, but only came in and out of the barbershop in between hanging around the neighborhood with their friends.

Still, Lil' Rall and I did have a tradition. Each weekend he came by, he would teach me how to play chess. Chess was one of those barbershop games for the folks who would stop in every day but never get a haircut. Come to think of it, the barbershop was like a lounge. A men's-only club. Each week, Lil' Rall would play a few games with me, teaching me how the board and each piece worked. Pawns could only move one space at a time. The rook could move several spaces vertically or horizontally. The bishop could move several spaces diagonally. The knight could move in an L shape. The king was the piece everyone was protecting, as it could move only one space, and the queen was the most powerful piece on the board, moving in any direction she wanted.

From week to week, I would improve. I was able to beat a few of the other men who I would play with from time to time, but never Lil' Rall. To be fair, there was a part of me that never *wanted* to beat Lil' Rall. Even if I knew I had a better move on the board, I would make the wrong one. In some weird way it was important that he stayed the teacher and I the student. Maybe I felt that if he knew I needed to learn from him, he wouldn't leave us.

In 1994, Rall and Rasul's younger brother, Justice Dwight Elder, was born. Uncle was now in his thirties, so his parenting was a lot different. He was a business owner, had a few side hustles, and was much more involved as a father this go-around. However, Justice was bad as hell—he knew that he could practically get his way with anything he wanted. But overall, Rall and Rasul reacted pretty well to having a younger brother. Lil' Rall was a natural nurturer, so he stepped right into that role of babysitter when needed. Rasul was cool with Justice, too. I think because they were teens, though, they were more concerned with spending time with girls.

Now that Justice was the youngest grandchild, Garrett was no longer the baby...unless you asked Garrett. Justice would be in the shop from time to time with Lil' Rall, babysitting once again, but the foursome remained the foursome, each of us with our own barbershop memories. It's clear that barbershop life is a communal story.

Barbershops are a staple of the Black community. In many ways, the barbershop can be a safe place for Black boys and cultivate an environment of learning and growth. Many Black barbershops now have literacy programs, where young kids can pick up a book before they sit in the chair or are even required to read a book while actually getting their haircut. Barbering is an accessible job for many formerly incarcerated Black men who have dealt with issues around joining the workforce. It has provided a means of income for Black men to take care of the needs of their families and communities. Many Black barbershops participate in yearly community-service efforts to groom men who may not be able to afford those services.

However, the barbershop can also be a place of trauma. In many ways, the barbershop bred masculinity as a goal, with achievement intertwined with misogyny and homophobia. Although the word was never directed toward me, the word "faggot" was a staple. Not just in that barbershop, but in every barbershop I've ever visited. If you stayed a customer long enough, you would hear someone use the f-word. And it had so many variations. Some used it to describe a person who was actually gay or who they thought was gay. More often, though, it was used to describe "softness," femininity, or effeminate behaviors.

One example would be the weekly fights over the Dallas Cowboys. If the guys got to arguing in that barbershop about Deion Sanders, someone was going to use the f-word to describe him. Deion was an amazing athlete, and he was also very well groomed. This was before terms like "metrosexual"—a word created in the early 2000s to describe men like Jay-Z and Diddy, who used to get manicures and facials and practiced grooming habits without a questioning of their sexuality. These qualities were all seen as signs of being too feminine— and homophobia is a by-product of misogyny.

Misogyny wasn't just in the language they used but also in the way the men treated women. If you were a woman walking by in the shop, they were going to look at your ass. And after you left, they were going to talk about what they would do to your ass. And don't let a fine woman walk by the shop window—folks would jump up and run outside just to harass her.

Be clear on the language I'm using when I say "harass," because that is what it was. No one was walking past that shop to gain attention or be chased down the street. As a kid, I saw this behavior as what men would do when they were attracted to a woman. It was normalized in music videos and in my real life. When a woman said, "No thanks, I'm good," she should've been left alone. But that rarely happened.

As an adult, I know the potential danger when a woman rejects a man's advances. Men perceive it as a threat to their manhood, and in many instances women have been harmed or even killed simply for not giving a man their phone number. As boys, we're conditioned to think manhood is achieved through sexual prowess and one's ability to court girls and women. Watching men act in this way was our entry point. Watching men shame men who didn't act this way became a trigger and trauma for those of us who had no desire to be like that, or for people like me who were dealing with their sexual identity.

In 1997, Uncle decided to close up the shop and move the family to Virginia. Garrett and I had to find new barbers, and another piece of our weekly normal was no longer a constant. I was sad that Uncle was leaving, sad that there would be no more weekends or haircuts from him. That would be the end of our barbershop days.

I can say that I'll always love the many memories we made at the barbershop and beauty salon. There were the pictures Uncle used to take of designs and parts in our hair so that he could be reminded of his skills, and the times the four of us would get the same design so that we could be cool together. Black boys getting their haircuts in Black barbershops will likely be a staple forever. I just hope future generations of Black boys are groomed to have a respect for all Black lives, rather than become products of the patriarchal environment.

Dear Nanny,

I can't believe it took me so long to write this. It's a little hard to do, because I can't believe you are no longer here physically. I know you are still with me, though. We always bonded over your ladybug accessories, and every time I see a ladybug, I know it's you. I want you to know that I finally started learning how to cook, and I wish you could try my Cajun catfish—I think you would have liked it.

The year 2020 is a mess. You aren't missing much. I mean, there's this new virus out called corona, and, honestly, it's attempting to take everyone out of here. I think about how lucky we were to be able to celebrate your life in December, because if you had passed in 2020, we might not have had that same opportunity to celebrate you.

I was told by a wise person that a classy lady always knows when it's time to leave, and you were definitely a classy lady; in a weird way you left us right on time. I am comforted knowing that there is an extra angel in heaven looking out for us during this weird time. I think about our memories often. How we both loved our dogs. How we used to say we would one day attend the Westminster Dog Show at Madison Square Garden. And how you said dogs needed to go to church, too, to get their lessons. I now have a new puppy, and best believe I'm gonna make sure she gets her church lessons.

I don't want to be too long-winded, because I can become kind of mushy, but I love you and I thank you for all that you taught me. I want you to know that you are missed, but I know when you are near.

Love,
Your grandson Justice Dwight

6

911, What's Your Emergency?

Nannyism: "A lie ain't a side of the story.
It's a lie."

It was a regular day on the block of Lansdowne Terrace. The birds were chirping, the bees were buzzing, and the sun was shining brightly on another day of adventures for the Elder-Johnson clan. We were fortunate to live in a neighborhood where there were a lot of kids nearby. Because our school, Cook School, was in walking distance, many families with children our age were around.

Up the block from us lived this family of white kids. Now, be clear, when I say a family of white kids, it is because if you didn't know that they had a Black father, you wouldn't know that they were half-Black. Hell, one of them even had red hair. There were four of them, just like there were four of us. Robert was the oldest, Daniel was second, Allison (the only girl) was the third, and Paul was the youngest. Nanny had a nickname for their clan. She used to say, "Y'all going up the street to play with White Willy and them?" We would say yes, and she would tell us to be careful.

There was a reason she told us to be cautious—she was a Black woman from the South. When she was growing up, her family had direct interactions with the Ku Klux Klan, and she knew all too well from her past just how unsafe interactions with white people could be.

This particular story about Lil' Rall, Rasul, and "White Willy and them" was passed down to me by Aunt Sarah, Nanny, and Rasul. When Lil' Rall and Rasul first moved to Plainfield in 1987, Lil' Rall was seven and Rasul had just turned six. I was still in the nursery in Nanny's basement, and Garrett was a month away from joining the crew. That summer before they started at Cook School, Nanny signed Lil' Rall and Rasul up for baseball. Baseball practice used to take place at the school's field. At the time, the team also included Robert, Daniel, Allison, and a few other kids. Even at a young age, Lil' Rall and Rasul were very good at baseball. This was also their first time around white kids. Growing up in the projects, they knew only Black kids, and specifically Black kids who might've witnessed and been involved in a lot of things that children shouldn't have. They saw plenty of fights, and they wanted to fight, too—cyclical learning. Plainfield was an adjustment for them, but Nanny did the best she could to show them how to operate in a new environment. She felt baseball would introduce them to new friends and help them acclimate to a different way of life.

This one day at baseball practice, the coach was running late, so the kids were unsupervised on the bench, with a few of the parents waiting in the stands. Rasul got thirsty while sitting in the summer heat and decided to take a five-minute walk back to the house for a Pepsi. Lil' Rall was still there, so Rasul left his equipment—including his cleats and glove—while he made the quick trip to Nanny's house. Rasul was always strong willed in that way. If a thought popped in his mind, he was certainly going to act on it. This independent mind often put Rasul at odds with us and, at times, even Nanny.

Falling between me and Lil' Rall couldn't have been easy for Rasul. He never felt seen, which made him do things to *be* seen. I also think Rasul longed for the love of his parents differently than Lil' Rall. Lil' Rall just suppressed it—the trauma, the hurt, the past—and moved on with what he had. Rasul, on the other hand, needed the love of his parents—a love he deserved. No matter how much love my aunts and Nanny poured into him, he still needed more.

There was also an imbalance of power in our little group. For me and Garrett, it was easy to follow the commands of Lil' Rall because he was five and eight years our senior, respectively. But Lil' Rall and Rasul were only seventeen months apart. A nine-year-old learning that a ten-year-old is in charge, simply because he is *slightly* older, didn't cut it for Rasul.

Looking back, I can see Rasul's side. Now, don't get me wrong, he knew how to cut up and stir the pot. But, had Rasul been put in charge even just a few times, his whole outlook on things could've been different. An older brother can be an overbearing thing to deal with, especially when you feel no one hears or sees you. And it's even harder when folks are always comparing you and setting expectations that remove your individuality. I wish Rasul knew just how seen he was. Just how loved he was. We all required a different type of care from Nanny, but she was only one woman, trying to create love with specificity to each of us, with no real blueprint. She did the best she could, and that was more than enough—even if it took some of us longer than others to know it. One thing we do know is, Rasul's ass wasn't supposed to leave that practice.

Yet and still, Rasul was going to do Rasul, so he started walking. While Rasul was gone, Allison decided to be funny—she placed his glove over her cleats and pretended she couldn't find them. Her mother then began looking for the cleats and found them under Rasul's glove. Allison, rather than admitting she hid them, said, "Rasul took them from me!"

By this point, Rasul had gotten his Pepsi and was heading back to the baseball field, hoping the coach had finally arrived. Nanny's house was around the corner from the entrance of the field. Rasul was still about fifty feet away when he saw Mrs. Todd walking up with Allison's cleats in hand.

"You tried to steal my daughter's cleats!"

Rasul, still holding a Pepsi and lost on what she was talking about, responded, "I didn't steal anything!"

By this point, Mrs. Todd was hysterically yelling at him. As an adult, Rasul often talks about this moment: He knew he was Black, but this was the moment he realized what being a Black kid meant—when white folks assumed the worst about you. As he put it years later, "There was never a doubt in her mind that I wasn't a thief, because it made more sense to her for a Black kid to steal than for her daughter to tell a lie."

Fortunately for Rasul, Nanny happened to be close enough to her front door, which was open with the screen door closed, meaning she could hear everything happening a block or two away. This lady was so loud that she could be heard up the street by Nanny—mind you, she was an adult berating a six-year-old child that she was *not* kin to. Nanny walked outside, saw who it was, and immediately started marching over toward them.

Be clear, Nanny was a Black woman born during Jim Crow in South Carolina. She fully knew the implications of racism and power dynamics of white women, as she had been there before with her own children. As a little girl, my mom would come home from school saying she was "dirty." This was right after *Brown v. Board of Education* and schools were integrated. One day Nanny finally asked her, "Who is saying you are dirty?" When my mom said it was the white kids, Nanny realized that those children had never been around anyone with Black skin, so they thought my mother's skin color meant she was unclean. Furthermore, she could only imagine the other, deeper parallels the families of those white children drew between being Black and being "dirty."

A few years after that, Nanny dealt with another situation that bore even more similarities to the incident with Rasul and Allison's mother. When Aunt Sarah was a little girl in the late '60s, she befriended a white girl who lived up the street from them. Although the little white girl had no issues with Aunt Sarah, her older brother did have an issue with her playing with a Black friend.

One day, Aunt Sarah went up the street to her friend's house. The brother opened the door and told her to come in, but when she attempted to enter, the boy slammed the door into Aunt Sarah's face. Aunt Sarah went running back home to Nanny. When she explained what had happened, Nanny went up that street and knocked on that door.

When the door opened, she walked right in that house and asked who slammed the door on her daughter's face. Aggressively, the boy's mother tried to kick her out the house and put a finger up in Nanny's face. One thing we *all* knew was, if you put your finger up in Nanny's face, then you better be ready to fight. Nanny coldcocked her. The husband came down the steps and before he could even run up on her, she clocked him, too.

"Don't you *ever* hit my daughter in the face again."

According to our family's stories, the cops were called and Nanny was charged with assault but didn't face arrest. However, she had to appear in court to defend against the charge. The mother she hit claimed that she had a miscarriage from the assault. But by the time it went to court, there was no proof that the woman was ever pregnant. Nanny paid a fine and the ordeal was over. Fast-forward nearly twenty years, and here she was again. Just like two decades prior, she knew she had business to handle.

As Nanny got closer to Allison's mother, she yelled, "Stop yelling at my grandson!"

"Your grandson stole my daughter's shoes," Mrs. Todd yelled back.

By now, Nanny stood between Mrs. Todd and Rasul to protect him from her. However, this didn't stop her aggressive gesturing toward Rasul. Unfortunately, she didn't know that Nanny would rely on more than her words, especially if she felt threatened. Midsentence, Nanny came up underneath Mrs. Todd's chin with an uppercut worthy of winning the heavyweight title. And down went Mrs. Todd. Before she walked back home, Nanny told Rasul to go on back to practice and come get her if anyone else started with him or Lil' Rall.

Now, this is where the story really takes flight. A few minutes later, a call came in to the 911 desk in Plainfield.

"Nine-one-one, what's your emergency?" said the female operator.

"There's a Black woman up here slapping white women!"

"Okay, can you give a street of where the incident occurred?" said the operator.

"The intersection of Lansdowne Terrace and Marshall Place." The operator's heart started racing. She took a breath and said, "Okay, we will send an officer out that way."

The operator immediately called the police department, but not for an officer. She needed to talk to her sister, who was head of secretaries at the station. As you can guess, the 911 call came in to Aunt Sarah—one of Nanny's daughters. And as soon as she heard it was a Black woman on that block slapping white women, she decided to call my mother at the police department.

"Kaye!" Aunt Sarah said. "I think Mommy slapped up Mrs. Todd up the block from her. Call Gregory and get him over."

My mother contacted my father, a cop in the Plainfield Police Division. He and another officer went out to the scene to respond to the call. Mrs. Todd was back at her house when the cop car pulled up to the scene.

Nanny was home, while Lil' Rall and Rasul were still at practice. There are always a few sides to the story. Their side, your side, and somewhere in the middle—the truth. Of course, Mrs. Todd's story left out the part about her accosting a six-year-old Black child and made it seem like Nanny hit her unprovoked. Afterward, my dad went over to Nanny's house and she told him exactly what had happened.

"She was threatening your nephew, so I handled it."

Nanny and my father were always on the same page when it came to protecting the family, and that definitely included Lil' Rall and Rasul, who had just moved to Plainfield under everyone's watchful eye. Under any other circumstances, Nanny would have been arrested, had we not had so many connections within the department—which speaks volumes about the ways policing can easily be manipulated. In the end, Nanny was issued a desk ticket, so she and Rasul still had to appear in court. Rasul always talks about going to court that day. He still remembers being nervous, seeing the judge, and having to talk about what happened. But what he remembers most is the trauma of going through all of this for something he didn't even do. He remembers that his Nanny had to protect him from something that was a lie to begin with.

Nanny ended up getting probation in lieu of jail time, as long as she completed her required community-service hours and paid a fine. To this day we are pretty sure that Nanny paid her fine, but we know for a fact that she did not complete her community service. One of the running family jokes from Aunt Sarah was the constant reminder: "One of these days they gonna come with a warrant and arrest you. *They put old people in jail!*"

"I wish they would try," Nanny would always respond. "I would shoot them first."

I often think about "Karen," the colloquial term used to describe a white woman who manipulates the police into wrongfully arresting or harming a Black person. White women weaponizing their whiteness has historical precedence and has gotten many a Black person killed. America has always operated under a "damsel in distress" syndrome, a notion of white women being helpless, innocent, and needing rescue by white men. Those white men have historically enacted violence on the Black community at the behest of these women, whether or not the original stories they told were true. Even today, many of these saviors are police officers and agents of the state who perpetuate systems that benefit white supremacy.

I'm big on connecting the events of my past to those of my ancestors. For example, there's the story of a young Black boy named Emmett Till, who was lied on by a white woman named Carolyn Bryant for "whistling" at her. In the summer of 1955, he was dragged out of his relatives' home by Roy Bryant and J. W. Milam, the white men she lied to, and was severely beaten to death. Emmett Till was a fourteen-year-old Black child. When his body was recovered, he had been tortured so badly that one could barely recognize his face. Rather than have a closed-casket ceremony, his mother, Mamie Till, left the casket open so that the world could see how heinous white violence was. She fought because she knew her son did nothing wrong and was killed for being Black. Even today, there is a deep fear when Black children leave the home and have to survive in a world intent on killing them.

Nanny knew that Allison's mother was wrong. She knew Rasul had no reason to steal some little girl's

cleats, especially since she was able to provide everything her grandchildren needed. Mrs. Todd learned a
valuable lesson that day, though. The new kids on the
block weren't going anywhere, and the next time she
thought about talking to them any kind of way, Nanny
was going to be right there to check her again.

Funny enough, the relationship between the four
of us boys and "White Willy and them" improved after
that. Regardless of their mother's behavior, their dad
was an older Black man who was set on making his kids
understand that they had privileges other Black kids
didn't. There were times when he would tell them in
front of us that, while they were half-Black, they pre-
sented as white, and that meant society had a different
set of rules for them. After the day on the baseball field,
we all grew very, very close. Lil' Rall and Rasul became
best friends with Robert and Daniel. Paul and I were
the same age, so we became best friends, too. Garrett,
although the youngest, would hang with Paul and me, or
the whole group. Allison was cool and always around,
although at times she could be a bit overdramatic.

Overall, the lesson in this is how we dealt with
racism as young boys. Even if we couldn't name it,

we knew how it made us feel. We could process how quickly we could be seen as nefarious, as opposed to the white children, who were presumed innocent, even if proven guilty. And today I realize what Black parents must think about when sending their kids out into a world that is dangerous, especially when they can't be there to protect every action—or know that their presence still can't protect them.

We were fortunate that day. We were fortunate many days. However, the experience of that never goes away. It didn't go away for Rasul and it certainly never went away for Nanny. However, our resilience is continuing to find joy in spite of it all.

Play ball!

I love you, Nanny.

Thank you for giving me a real childhood.

Thank you for spoiling us and teaching us hard work and discipline.

Thank you for showing us the other side of life and teaching us the hustle spirit.

I am a recipient of great favor,

Like a castaway's graduation to a trailblazer,

Like a child's journey to adulthood.

I was an asteroid. I needed the space to birth a crater.

My fight was labor.

Now I'm the lake and the ice skater.

And you, a bottomless glacier in all of her grandeur.

Much deeper than cold, like an anti-hero,

And just like you.

You have melted and this hurt the world,

Like the elephant left the room to flap
its wings.

You said the prayers,

We memorized the measures.

I took the dares.

I found the danger.

Escaped the lairs.

Retraced the steps and paced the stairs.

Kevin is there. Hope is there. So is Lil'
Kevin.

Flowers await patiently,

Long before despair.

I left with nothing.

As long as I breathe,

I'll be your air.

I'll gather our share.

My mother. My dad is in there.

Time packed the despair.

How much room would remain in this
apartment,

If I unpacked this here?

Would this letter be the same when the
deadline came?

I can't compare.

All the boxes just setting square

in my family room. They shrink on the shelf.

I don't drink of myself. I am the well.

I am alive and well. I am well.

Non-investors have failed.

I have stumbled and prevailed. I am well, with buckets to bail.

Cinderella in this tale. Stayed passed twelve.

Dancing on the glass ceiling.

Straight from the attic.

Let's be frank,

I should unpack these boxes,

Clear the attic and garages.

Free the little boy hostage. I still fight boxing.

But I got this.

And you got me.

I love you, Nanny.

Sul

7

Did We Kill Matt?

Nannyism: "Y'all are all y'all got."

Every kid lives for that one special moment every year, after the weather has changed from the showers of April to the flowers blooming in May to the heat wave that comes every June. It's a magical time for a kid, when it's hot all day and hot all night, and there is nothing to wake up to every morning but the thought of what new adventures the day will bring. That one special moment? The last day of school.

Every year, the final day of school was a ceremonious

occasion. Despite teachers giving us "summer reading"—a three-book requirement that we *all* waited till the last two weeks of summer to finish—it was three months of no homework and no real responsibilities.

Summers for the Johnson-Elder clan were pretty simple during those times. Most days, my mother would wake me and Garrett and get us ready to go to Nanny's house. Oftentimes, she would pack a bag for the week, and we would just live there. It was always much easier to keep me, Lil' Rall, Rasul, and Garrett in one place, with Lil' Rall and Uncle Kevin alternating as the babysitters.

There were certain things we knew we would do every summer. For example, about twenty minutes from our house was a small family-owned amusement park called Bowcraft. It had miniature roller coasters and rides, similar to those of a carnival. If we had been good that week—meaning no fights and foolishness—Nanny would take us there for several hours. We also took one big vacation every summer. Whether it was driving down the East Coast with several stops along the way or flying across the country to California, Nanny made sure that we saw life outside Plainfield.

Nanny traveled often with our parents when they were younger, and it was a tradition that she continued with us. There are many Black kids who rarely have the chance to see what's outside their city or state, who never really travel and step outside their environments. We were fortunate to be able to "see some world," as they would say.

But the highlights of every Black summer were the family cookouts. We were a big family, so there were multiple cookouts every year. These events often combined Nanny's side with Old Daddy's people. It was the perfect blend of families, with all of us raised more like brothers and sisters than just cousins. That Black-family thing where your parents' first cousins become your "aunts and uncles" by proxy was a sign of respect in our community in many ways.

In Plainfield, we had an annual Fourth of July parade that was one of the oldest and largest in the state. So, in addition to going to the parade with Nanny, we would also have a cookout to commemorate the holiday. This one year, we decided to have a big family cookout at Liberty State Park. The park is located on the Jersey side of the Upper New York Bay, directly across from

Ellis Island, Liberty Island, and the majestic Statue of Liberty. Liberty State Park was full of bike-riding trails, walking trails, and large cookout areas where you could play music and games with the family.

Us four boys were really excited to be out there that day. It was interesting, because one would assume you'd tire of sharing your toys, time, and space every day. Instead, we loved being together. Every day was a chance for us to set something on fire or ride our bikes to the parts of town where we were told we couldn't, or curse because there were no adults around. Beneath all the fighting and roughhousing was our undying love for one another. The type of love that says, "I can beat you up, but if anyone lays a hand on you, we are *all* beating them up." The type of love where they never saw me differently because of how effeminate I was, although other kids made jokes (but not too many, because Lil' Rall and Rasul would fight them for talking about me). The type of love that means the term "cousin" isn't powerful enough. Unconditional love. We knew that we truly were all that we had, and this day put our love to the test.

It was a typical hot summer afternoon in July, with

all the young cousins getting together to play cards, sack-toss, and anything else we could come up with. At around six PM, Lil' Rall and Rasul asked for permission to go down the paved walkway to the nearby landing, where kids often skipped rocks across the water. Nanny agreed, but instructed us to keep an eye out for each other.

Earlier during the summer, Lil' Rall and Rasul taught me the basics at the Cook School Pond by the Big Yellow House, but I wasn't skilled quite yet. Lil' Rall and Rasul could easily get a rock to skip four or five times before it finally sank. This was probably one of the only things Rasul was better at than Lil' Rall. Garrett was still younger and just had fun throwing rocks, even if they immediately sank. But for me, I always desired to be as good as, or better than, Lil' Rall and Rasul at everything. Most times I could only skip a rock across the water once or twice. Although that would frustrate me, Lil' Rall and Rasul always encouraged me to keep trying. Every now and then, I could get a rock to skip four or five times, and their excitement made me feel good about myself. For a boy who was dealing with identity issues from a very young age, they always knew how to include me like I was "one of the boys."

After Lil' Rall, Rasul, Garrett, and I took the long walk up the trail of Liberty State Park that July day, we reached the part where the rocks met the water. Think of it as a beach full of pebbles and stones. Not a huge beach but just a little section, maybe about a quarter the size of a football field. A few people were sitting where there was more sand than rocks.

As adventurous kids, we decided we were going to see who could skip a rock the farthest. We all started taking turns, standing about twenty feet back from the water. Of course, this made it much harder to get them to skip, but we also wanted to make sure we were a safe distance away, as this wasn't a pond but an actual body of water. We all threw rocks for a few minutes, most of them skipping only once or twice.

After a while, I got frustrated—I still had that desire to beat my cousins. At that moment, I decided to get a little closer to skip my next rock. I walked down toward the water, maybe about ten feet in front of all my cousins. Once I reached the spot I wanted to throw from, I saw the *perfect* rock. It was a flattie—an oval-shaped rock with a flat, smooth surface. Flatties were always the best rocks to use. They fit perfectly in the hand and would jump across the water like a frog from lily pad to lily pad. I picked it up and threw it, and it skipped across the water once, twice, three times, and...sank. Still, I was so happy to have gotten three skips!

My pure joy made me forget everything that was happening around me, including the danger that lay just ten feet behind me. On the ground in front of me, I saw another good rock to throw. I bent down to pick it up, but before I knew it, everything was black.

Apparently, when I bent down to grab that rock, Lil' Rall had thrown his own toward the water before seeing me. His rock hit the upper right side of my head and immediately knocked me unconscious. The other cousins who had accompanied the four of us panicked and screamed, as did onlookers. I, of course, don't remember any of this because I was laid out on the ground, knocked out.

Lil' Rall and Rasul came over and found me bleeding profusely from my head. They shook me and tried to wake me up, but I was out cold. Lil' Rall and Rasul picked me up, Lil' Rall under my right arm and Rasul under my left. The two of them, ages twelve and thirteen, began carrying my limp eight-year-old body back toward the cookout. It must've felt like an eternity for them. I can't even imagine what thoughts were going through their minds as they carried me up this long walkway while blood ran down my face. Well, I do know one thought, because years later they told me, "We thought we killed you, Matt."

I remember finally starting to come to, although things were a bit hazy. We were still a bit away from where the cookout was taking place, but I could see the family in the distance.

"Matt!" Rasul yelped.

"What happened?" I replied as they both continued carrying me.

"Matt, move your legs," Lil' Rall said. "We gotta get you to an ambulance."

I looked down and saw all the blood on my shirt. My face felt sticky in the summer heat as the blood began to dry. Surprisingly, I didn't panic. My adrenaline was running so high that I didn't even feel any pain. I just began moving my feet in unison with the quick steps of Lil' Rall and Rasul as the family came into view.

Once we were closer, Lil' Rall exclaimed, "*Help,*

Matt is hurt!" The family saw all the blood, and everyone immediately started shouting.

"Oh, my God!"

"MATT!"

Nanny hopped up from her lawn chair and screamed, "What happened?"

Lil' Rall and Rasul began explaining how the whole accident occurred when we were skipping rocks. They feared they were in trouble, but Nanny quickly reassured them that everything was okay.

"Get me some paper towels," she yelled.

Someone in the family handed her some, and she sat down in the lawn chair while I sat on her lap. I laid my head against her chest as she held the towels to my head to stop the bleeding. "We called for the ambulance, Louise," my uncle Mack stated.

A few minutes went by before the ambulance pulled up. They came out and started checking me and asking questions. Because I had been unconscious for a few minutes, they decided to take me in and confirmed that I would need stitches. The EMTs helped me climb into the back of the truck, and I sat down on the metal bench attached to the wall.

"Who is riding with him?" the EMTs asked.

Before Nanny could open her mouth, my aunt Joanne jumped up and said, "I'm gonna ride with my baby Matt."

You could've fried an egg on Nanny's forehead from how hot she got. Aunt Joanne is Nanny's sister-in-law once removed. I'm kidding about the once-removed part, as I have no idea what that means when people say it. Suffice it to say, Old Daddy's brother, my uncle Horace, was married to Aunt Joanne, making her and Nanny sisters-in-law, until Joanne and Horace got divorced. Even with the divorce, Aunt Joanne still stayed in the family, and is still the cool loudmouth aunt from Jersey City. A heavyset brown-skinned Black woman with a Jheri curl and a bit of rasp to her voice.

Nanny and Joanne always had a good relationship, so there was no beef. However, Nanny's grandkids were *Nanny's* grandkids. And everyone knew that no decision was *ever* to be made involving Lil' Rall, Rasul, Matt, or Garrett that hadn't been run by, edited, voted on, and approved by Louise Kennedy Evans Elder. Nanny would've probably cursed Aunt Joanne out, but I was already going through enough at the moment and she didn't want to make any more of a scene.

"Okay, Joanne, ride with Matt," Nanny said before turning to me. "Matt, I'm following right behind the ambulance. I'll see you at the hospital."

"Okay, Nanny," I said as they closed the doors.

I sat next to Aunt Joanne as she held my hand for the fifteen-minute ride to the hospital. By now the adrenaline had started to come down, which meant the pain was starting to come up. Even in the midst of all of this, I couldn't stop thinking about how cool the experience was. There was something about being a boy that led me to believe all of this was some rite of passage into manhood. Broken bones, blood, sirens—this was everything I'd imagined. It was like my own little adventure. What would stitches be like? Would I get to show them off to the other kids we hung out with? Did this mean that I would finally be seen as tough? Would I need brain surgery? For an eight-year-old, these were the thoughts that ran through my head from zero to one hundred in ridiculous fashion.

The sirens finally stopped as we pulled up to the

emergency room. The back doors opened, and they got Aunt Joanne out first. The EMT then helped me climb down. Aunt Joanne went up to the counter and told them the basics. She let them know that my grandmother was coming in a few and would provide my insurance information.

They opened the double doors and I proceeded to a hallway, where we sat in two chairs and waited for the doctor to call us back. Now, I'll be honest, this part gets funny in my mind and I don't quite remember when the switch-off happened, but after a few minutes, Aunt Joanne was no longer the one sitting beside me and it was Nanny holding my hand as we waited for the doctor. I'm not even sure how Aunt Joanne got home.

The doctor finally called us to come back. We went into the room and he had a metal tray set up with string, a hook, and a needle. My eyes got really big looking at the equipment. Now I was getting nervous. I must've squeezed Nanny's hand tighter because the next thing I heard was, "It's gonna be okay, Matt. I'm right here." I looked up at her and nodded. The doctor helped me jump up on the table and told me to lie down. Nanny was to my left and the doctor was standing over me to my right.

"Okay, Matt," the doctor said, "here is the needle. I know it looks big, but the whole thing isn't going in. It's going to pinch a little, but I have to numb you, so you don't feel the stitches going in, okay?"

I looked at the doctor and said, "Okay." Nanny was still holding my hand.

I saw the needle and closed my eyes hard. I could feel a little pinch. Then another little pinch. The doctor said, "Okay, one more," and I felt one last pinch. I opened my eyes and let out a deep breath. Apparently, I was holding it the whole time.

"You okay, Matt?" Nanny asked.

"Yeah, it didn't hurt that bad," I replied.

"Okay," the doctor said. "I'm going to give you a few minutes so it gets numb, and then I'm going to stitch up the wound. What color do want? I have red, green, yellow, or blue."

I instantly brightened—everything was becoming cool again. I survived being hit with a rock. I survived all the bleeding. I survived the needle, and now I was getting fun-colored stitches that would be my badge of honor.

"I'll take the blue ones."

He pulled out the blue thread of sutures and looped it into the hook needle. I took a deep breath. The doctor told me to close my eyes and count back from one hundred.

"Ready, Matt?" Nanny asked. Then she started counting. "One hundred, ninety-nine, ninety-eight…" and I began counting along with her. I had my eyes closed the whole time, but I could feel the pressure of the stitches going in and out. I didn't feel any pain, though. I just kept counting backward and wondering what it would look like when it was done. "Fifteen, fourteen, thirteen…" I kept counting. "Five, four, three, two, one, zero…" as I opened my eyes.

The doctor was already taking his gloves off. "Okay, Matt. You're done. There's a mirror over there if you want to see what it looks like."

Nanny helped me get off the table, and I walked over to my reflection. Blood all over my shirt. And four stitches in the top right corner of my head with a neon blue color. I was tough, and all I could think about was showing Lil' Rall and Rasul.

Nanny asked me, "You wanna go home or you wanna stay with your cousins tonight?"

I told her that I wanted to stay with Lil' Rall and

Rasul. We walked out of the hospital together and drove back to Plainfield, where my cousins had been living with their dad and stepmom—Uncle and Aunt Crystal. By now, the sun had set and I just looked out the front-seat window of the station wagon.

When we finally got to Lil' Rall and Rasul's, the two of them ran down from their room, met me halfway in the hallway, and the three of us hugged.

"Matt," Rasul said, "I thought we had killed you!"

I laughed and said, "Look, I got stitches!"

Nanny made sure she told Uncle and Aunt Crystal to just keep an eye on me and check in case anything changed. The three of us boys went back into Lil' Rall and Rasul's room. I sat down on the edge of their bunk bed and told them about everything, from the ambulance ride to getting the stitches. They were so proud of me, they let me choose the video game we would play that night. We easily stayed up till three AM, playing and just having a good time. It was truly another one of those days that would become a story to tell our kids, nieces, and nephews when we became the adults at the cookout.

There was a magic that night, a bond formed through a shared experience. We were becoming the group of boys that our uncles once were with their cousins, and that their parents once were with their cousins, and so on and so on. We were continuing the legacy of Black-boy joy. The spirit of kids being allowed to be kids.

That story remains one of my favorite memories because it is a reminder of love. My cousins and I didn't get along all the time, but that day was all about their love for me and the fear of what could have happened. It was about Nanny holding my hand, as I'm sure she had held the hand of many before. My nurturing Black grandmother who put her own worries to the side to make sure her baby was okay.

We have all heard the saying about how "big boys don't cry," a mentality that continues to harden us. But that day, there wasn't some big push to "tough it out." The first reaction wasn't for me and my cousins to dap, or handshake, but to run to one another and hug. There was never any shortage of love between us. I'm grateful that we, as Black boys, had moments to be vulnerable, moments to be soft.

MATT TO NANNY

Dear Nanny,

I knew this day would come—the day when your physical body had served its purpose here on Earth and you became that magical, spiritual power we could call on to remind us of our faith and cover us with blessings and prayers from the other side.

You were more than just a grandmother to me. You did all the grandma things, of course—the Christmas gifts, the birthday gifts, the big hugs whenever I saw you. The amazing food you would cook for us, as both kids and adults. You were a matriarch unlike any other. But the most important thing you were to me, and to all of us, was a companion. In losing you, I didn't lose just a grandmother—I lost one of my best friends. That's been the hardest thing for me to process. Blood makes you family, but it's the relationships you build that make it special and something different. Something magical. Something Black and joyous. That's what we had.

It wasn't until I was older that I realized how much time you and I spent together over my adolescent years. Every Saturday, I was your flea market partner. You would pay me five dollars an hour to set up our section and help you sell odds and ends. And on Sundays—when we didn't go to church—we would do the same thing again. It was our time. I learned the art of the hustle, how to sell and make my own money, and it's something I still do to this day. Eventually, I even became your banker and sat in your room counting all the hidden envelopes of money you kept in case of emergencies.

Do you remember when we started the soup kitchen? Friday nights we would go to the church and prepare the food together. As the soup cooked over the stove, we would stay up and play rummy 500 until one AM. Afterward, we would package and store everything in the church fridge. The next morning, we would return and make deliveries to the sick and shut in throughout the city of Plainfield. You taught me how to be an activist and care for my community from a young age.

You were my constant. You were the person we could all go to if we had a problem that needed to be fixed, the person we could come to for breakfast before work and for dinner after. Even as we got older, you were still such a cool lady. You were seventy when you bought a huge pickup truck. Who does that? Driving through the city with a purple church hat and one hand on the steering wheel! I'm really going to miss your earthly being, although I know I can call on your spirit whenever I need.

Do you remember the conversation we had in the hospital a few months before you passed? I don't even think you know how powerful your words were that day. They were words that the five-year-old boy who knew he was "different" finally needed to hear so that he could be free—words that the thirty-three-year-old man sitting in front of you that day also needed to finally be free.

You looked at me and said, "Matt. You not just gay, right?"

I looked up at you while giggling and said, "No, I'm not just gay."

"The ladies at the church always ask me 'Is Matt gay?' and I say, 'No, but if you want to know, ask him.'" I laughed some more, and then you said it. "You never really were a boy, but you also weren't a girl. You just always sat somewhere in the middle."

Your words were so simple yet so moving. My whole life, I feared accepting that I really didn't have a gender but that I existed as something I couldn't name. Thankfully, we now have the words and language I needed, and I can say I'm nonbinary. But it wasn't until then that I knew someone else saw it—my biggest fear. In that moment, it didn't matter anymore. I found the courage to be myself because I knew you knew and would protect me.

It took cancer six attempts to take you away from us. But little did cancer know that you were going to a place where it could no longer attack your body. A place of no pain, no sorrows, and no worries. Although I wish we could have kept you here, for some of the big blessings to come in our life, we had to let go of the biggest presence we all knew. Our family will never be the same without you. But we are stronger and better because of everything you taught us and everything we do on your behalf.

You didn't really die. Real ones never die.

I've come to realize you are very much alive, just in a different form. I still talk to you out loud. Still laugh when I write your stories. When I speak your name, I get chill bumps, letting me know that you are still here. And in the moments when it's really, really quiet? I can hear you. I can hear you.

I've told your stories, and now you will live on forever in the thoughts and minds of so many. Thank you for everything you did for us, especially your grandsons you raised together. Oh, and we know Kennedy and Garrett are your favorite grandchildren, but it won't stop us from arguing about it every holiday.

Love,
Matt (George)

New Home, New Beginnings

Nannyism: "Scared money don't
make money."

As the saying goes, all good things must come to an end, and so did the adventures in the Big Yellow House at 1241 Lansdowne Terrace. It was 1993 when things started to change for the better or worse, depending on how you looked at it. Everyone had to make some tough decisions. But as Nanny would say, "Scared money don't make money." Meaning, if you are afraid to invest your money, time, and energy, you will never know what you may have achieved or learned. You can't be afraid to invest in yourself—even if you lose, there is a lesson in the loss and a greater reward, should your investment in yourself pay off. Self-doubt can lead you to a place where you don't take a chance on a dream, and Nanny taught us that you couldn't be scared to go out in the world and follow your passions, even if it came with some risks.

Nanny had many jobs and did many different things in her life. Some decisions worked out and some didn't. But she learned a lesson from each one that helped her navigate whatever she did next. Nineteen ninety-three was the year that everyone had to take a chance on themselves and go "all in," as they say in poker.

In the Big Yellow House, the mainstays were Uncle Kevin, Nanny, Aunt Munch, Lil' Rall, and Rasul. However, in 1993, Uncle Kevin finally decided he was going to make a start of his life without the help of Nanny. He moved down to Stone Mountain, Georgia, joining several other older cousins and uncles who moved there during the '90s to escape the dangers of New Jersey—the drugs, the thievery, and the people who were after them because of both. There is a somber pic of me, Rall, Rasul, and Garrett taking Uncle Kevin to the train station to leave. Every time I see that picture, I think of how bittersweet that day was. Another one of our constants was leaving us.

Meanwhile, Uncle finally decided to leave the street life alone and focus on his barbering and his side hustle, an art business through which he sold his own work and helped other artists sell their prints. These business endeavors meant he was more financially stable, and it was decided that Lil' Rall and Rasul would leave the Big Yellow House and move in with him and Aunt Crystal. It seemed everything was shifting so quickly.

After all these changes, just Aunt Munch and Nanny were left. So, Nanny decided it was time to downsize to a house with less rent and less space. That year, Nanny and Aunt Munch left the Big Yellow House and moved across town to 900 Lewis Avenue. They were still in Plainfield but farther from the school Garrett and I attended. That meant there would be some changes in where we went after class. Instead of heading to the Big Yellow House, my mother decided that we would go to a family friend's place instead. This adjustment for us was tough. Lil' Rall and Rasul were about twelve and thirteen and had moved on to middle school, leaving

Garrett and me behind at Cook Elementary School. And with Lil' Rall and Rasul living with their parents, the four of us no longer saw one another every day.

Nanny's new home was much smaller, a split-level with a decent-sized backyard and side yard. Still, the house just didn't have the same life as the other one. There were no Lil' Rall and Rasul to hang with. There weren't any neighborhood kids, either. The new side of town was extremely quiet, with no real traffic or main roads. There was no pond, no bike trails, no adventures. It was just a quiet, quaint house on the other side of town. Lewis Avenue still held all the holiday dinners and Nanny's big summer cookout, but it felt like a vacation home. The one good thing was the fact that most of the family still lived in the same city, just minutes apart, so we still spent many weekends together.

One of the first major events at the new house on Lewis Avenue was Uncle Rall and Aunt Crystal's wedding. When I think about it, though, I don't recall the moment I learned that they were getting married. I just remember being told that Rasul and I had to put on tuxedos and usher people into the house. The best men in the wedding were Lil' Rall and Garrett. The night before the ceremony, Garrett and I stayed at Uncle's house with Lil' Rall and Rasul. To be honest, I think we were all a little bit excited, even if we didn't understand what was going to take place. All we knew was that there would be a wedding in the living room of the new house the next day.

It was a chilly day in New Jersey on November 11, 1994. In the living room upstairs, we set up an arch for where Uncle and Aunt Crystal would exchange their vows. The arch sat in front of the big window that faced the street and the side yard of the house. We placed chairs extending from the living room into the dining room so that certain family members could sit. As instructed, Rasul and I walked everyone to their seats. One of my favorite pictures of all time is of Rasul and me looking up the stairs at the camera as we walked Nanny, the mother of the groom, to her seat. Even for a wedding in a house, it was put together with class and style.

The ceremony followed the same traditions as a normal wedding, as if the venue had been anywhere else. Uncle, Lil' Rall and Garrett walked in together and stood at the front of the living room. Aunt Crystal's daughter, Cierra, was the flower girl—the angry flower girl, to be fair, as she wasn't happy to wear that dress.

Before the bride came in, my mother and my aunt Darlene walked up to the platform landing where they did a duet of Patti LaBelle's "You Are My Friend." It was one of Nanny's favorite songs, as well as Aunt Crystal's. My mother and Aunt Darlene were church singers, and both of them hit every big note.

Aunt Crystal climbed the first flight of stairs as my mother and Aunt Darlene sang on the landing, before turning the corner to come up the next set of steps. She looked so pretty in her white dress. By this point, as tough as he was, Uncle was already crying. Aunt Crystal walked up to the front with him and they began the ceremony. It didn't take long, but it was intimate and special. It was the official introduction of Aunt Crystal into the family, as well as her daughter, Cierra.

After the ceremony, we all took pictures on the front lawn. People were driving by and honking and waving. It was November, so it was a little chilly outside, but the excitement of the event kept us all warm. There were pictures of all the boys with Uncle, pictures of us with the bride, pictures of our family becoming even bigger.

In many ways, it seemed like Lil' Rall and Rasul were on the way to the happy ending they always deserved. For many, it can be hard to find love once in life, and it seemed their father had found it twice. And with their father finding it a second time, they were getting the mother they needed. Someone who was caring, but cool and confident. Someone who was invested in seeing them be good people in the world. A woman in their daily lives, outside of my mom, my aunts, and Nanny.

Life on Lewis Avenue was slower than it was in the Big Yellow House—much quieter and more relaxed. During those years, we bonded with Nanny and one another as we evolved into young adults. Although the Lewis Avenue house was farther from our school, it was closer to my and Garrett's house and made summer visits easier. We would go to camp in the morning and then spend the rest of the day with Nanny. We played cards every day, rummy 500, for hours. She would come outside and play badminton with us on the side lawn. And on really hot days, she had this two-foot-high inflatable pool that we would sit in for hours. Those were the lazy days of summer with Nanny.

But I think our favorite part was the garden we started at the house. There was a patch of yard about ten feet long that extended from the back of the house. In the late spring, she'd bring us together for our yearly planting. "We gotta wait until there is no more frost at nights before we start," she would always say. We would be so eager come March and April, but she always knew the right time.

Every May, we would come over for a few hours and get our garden together. She bought tools for me and Garrett—little shovels and mini-rakes for us to dig up the grass so that we could get to the dirt. Then we would take the soil we purchased and lay it out fresh on top to create the bed to grow our vegetables. After, we would go to the store and decide which seeds we would buy. Nanny had been gardening for decades. It's one of those Black southern things I'm sure was passed down from her mother and her mother's mother, and Garrett and I were proud to take the "green thumb" of the family.

Much like the plants in the garden, we, too, continued to grow at the house on Lewis Avenue. We were no longer little kids, and did away with the little-kid

pleasures. Little did we know, the house was an important part of the transition to who we were becoming, the
shaping of our lives as we began the stages of puberty.
Whew, that's something I will definitely get into a little
later.

The new home proved that change is one of the
only constants in life. *Scared money don't make money.*
You can't have a different outcome if you aren't willing to invest in the unknown. I'm sure Nanny could've
made it work at the Big Yellow House, and I'm sure
Nanny wanted to keep Lil' Rall, Rasul, and the com-
fort of what our normal life had been for all those years.
But I also know she was never afraid to shake things up
a bit, knowing it was necessary for everyone's growth.
Nanny's changing up the environment allowed everyone to become responsible and to start making decisions
differently. Life wasn't always easy, and we still had our
regular Black family issues, but those years on Lewis
Avenue watered the garden of our family, with blooms
coming out on the other side.

GARRETT TO NANNY (SPOKEN AT HER FUNERAL)

Beauty rest.

She never said she was going to sleep. She always said she just needed her beauty rest.

I am the strong friend, the confidant, the bank, the vault, the security, the comforter. And at this point, I've consoled many others who mourned the loss of loved ones. Today, I don't have the words to console myself. How could the lady who instilled my faith in God, righted my wrongs, nurtured me, filled my stomach, and stood as my biggest fan be taken away from me?

Unfortunately, I never had any grandfathers to travel this journey of life with me, but Nanny didn't miss a beat in the maturation process as I became a man.

I remember the vacations she took us on as children, the graduations she attended front and center. When she felt trapped by doctors or her children, I was on speed dial to bail her out as she did for me.

Nanny was one of a kind. She gave all my friends a hard time and they loved her for it—each one of them has a memory or moment with her. She embraced my girlfriend Tiff as a granddaughter and they built their own relationship to the point that she sat in the delivery room and encouraged her to push, all while she was battling her own ailments.

She was always my biggest supporter. The day I was sworn in as a police officer, I remember the joy on her face. All she was saying was Old Daddy would be proud of you. But that wasn't what stood out to me. It was the look of fulfillment in her eyes, and how she wanted to share that moment with me. So, before I took my oath, I paused and I asked if she wanted to join me, my mom, and dad. She nodded her head yes. Behind that subtle motion, she couldn't be prouder that her baby boy was establishing himself in this world.

Now I gotta go through it without her. I know I'll be okay, because you got me, Nanny, just like you've always had.

Every year, I brought you flowers for Valentine's Day—even if it was my last bit of money—and that won't change. I just gotta bring them to you while you get your beauty rest.

I love you, Nanny!

What Happened to the Yams?

Nannyism: "If you use measuring cups, your food will taste measured. Taste your food while you cook it and adjust accordingly."

Picture it: New Jersey, 1999. It was finally the fourth Thursday in November—what most of us know as Thanksgiving, and easily the favorite holiday for the Elder-Johnson clan. It wasn't just the great fellowship, or the family going to the basement to watch the Thanksgiving game. It was all about the ridiculous amounts of food we would attempt to eat over a six-hour period, followed by *days* of amazing leftovers.

In Black families (and maybe in white families, but I wouldn't know), Thanksgiving dinner and Christmas dinner always had the oddest starting time. The other 363 days of the year, dinner for us would be between seven and nine PM. But on these holidays, we'd always attempt to start dinner at four thirty, which typically meant five thirty for everyone to finally arrive, and six for us to actually start eating. And every year we would keep up this terrible tradition of trying to start dinner on time and forever fail at it.

Nanny could cook anything she put her mind to. She was the only woman I know who could see something on TV and go in the kitchen and make it, as long as she had all the ingredients. She didn't even need to know the full recipe to make the meal come out just as it did on television. When I used to help her in the kitchen, I would ask her, "How do you cook without using measuring cups?"

"If you use measuring cups, your food will taste measured," she would say.

She always taught us that when you cook, you

should taste as you go along. Real cooking required care and attention to the food *while* you were cooking it. You can try a dish, realize it's missing something, and correct it while cooking. But if you wait until the end to taste it, you done messed up the whole meal. She followed her own advice about 99.9 percent of the time. But the one year she leaned into that 0.1 percent, we all paid for it.

Thanksgiving was her holiday and we all knew that. Her best dish was her famous mac and cheese, a recipe that had been passed down from Big Nanny to Grandma Lula Mae to Nanny and her sisters. The noodles were always seasoned perfectly, and they stuck together. There was always so much cheese, the perfect ratio. And be clear, mac and cheese is a side dish in Black families' homes. It goes *with* a meat—it is not the entire meal. And there was no such thing as "mac and cheese from a box," as Nanny would carry on.

When we were young, we had to sit at a separate dinner table from the adults called "the kids' table." It was always off to the side or in the basement or in another room away from the adults. The real reason we wanted to sit at the adults' table was because you got to listen to adult conversations. Also, it sucked being ten years old, eating with little cousins who may have been five or six and could barely feed themselves. The adult table was like the VIP section at the club. Every year you hoped for that nod signaling you were old enough to move up. But eventually all the cousins got older, so we were able to get rid of the notion of a kids' table and sit together to eat.

As for the menu, our Thanksgivings always had the same items:

Turkey, ham, Cornish hens, collard greens, mac and cheese, turnips, roast beef, pigs' feet (or as my dad would say, "trotters"), green beans, salmon, mashed potatoes, gravy, candied yams, and Nanny's famous sweet potato pies.

This particular Thanksgiving, I was about thirteen years old and we were all at my parents' house. My dad had this long wooden table that we brought out only twice a year—Thanksgiving and Christmas—that could seat up to twenty people. The table stretched so far across our living room that we had to move furniture around so everyone could fit. This was also the only time we ever broke out the fine china. A china cabinet was a source of pride that Nanny passed down. She grew up without much, so owning a hutch and at least one set of china was seen as an important marker and milestone.

This Thanksgiving had all the usual suspects: Aunt Sarah, Aunt Munch, me, Garrett, Rasul, my mom, my dad; the Jersey City crew of Aunt Margaret, Sean, Aunt Toni, Hope, some random friends; and, most important, Nanny. Lil' Rall was eighteen and away in the Air Force by this time, and Lil' Kevin was about eighteen and living with his mom in Jersey City.

We also had other people who would stop in throughout the night, but once enough family had shown up and my father started his chorus of "y'all niggas ready yet?" we were finally ready to eat. Everyone stood up in a circle and grabbed hands. One person would be called upon to pray over the food, usually my mother or my father.

"Bless the hands that prepared this food that we are about to receive for the nourishment of our bodies. In Jesus's name we pray, amen."

"Amen."

At that time, only the Lord knew how much prayer we'd need that year. After the prayer over the food, we all began to make our plates. My favorite was the ham, with all that brown-sugar glaze to go with my mac and cheese. Garrett's favorite was Nanny's famous mac and cheese. He could eat a plate of that on top of everything else. Rasul's favorite was Nanny's candied yams, and that day, he got a big helping.

People finally started to sit down and dig in. By this point the football game was on, so the only noise heard in between slurps and chomps was the TV. They say, "You can always tell when Black folks are eating, because no words are being spoken at all." Thanksgiving, for us, was devouring our first plate while already planning in our head what was going on the second one.

Everything was perfect, until Rasul sat down and finally got to dig his fork into those candied yams he had been waiting for for 364 days. Rasul's Cheshire cat grin quickly became a twisted face of ugly. We all looked at him as he said, with food in his mouth, "Someone get me a paper towel!" After getting the paper towel, he spit out the food.

"Rasul," Aunt Sarah asked him, "what's wrong with the food?"

"Something ain't right with the candied yams!"

Of course, like clockwork, we all took a taste of the candied yams and our faces twisted up as we chewed. Nanny came back into the room from the kitchen and Rasul jumped on her.

"Nanny! What did you do to the candied yams?"

She looked at us with this smile on her face and said, "I oranged them."

In unison, we all turned to her with our faces twisted and said, "You *oranged* them?"

She then looked at our inquisitive faces and explained her thought process behind changing up one of our favorite dishes over the last fifty years. "Well, I was watching Martha Stewart and she had a recipe to do orange candied yams. It looked good on television, so I wanted to experiment with it and see how it tasted."

I can't remember who said it, but the next statement was "Now, you *know* you can't take no soul food recipes from white people!" Everyone at the table laughed.

Funny enough, that next Thanksgiving she was being stubborn and tried a different flavoring in the yams...which I think was almond extract. Terrible again! For the rest of her life she only experimented dishes on us *before* Thanksgiving and never changed up her recipes for the big day again.

Suffice it to say, Black folks have a real connection with the foods we eat. As Black Americans, the food traditions we passed down, many originating from the South, are extremely important to our culture. As slaves, we ate the scraps, but our ancestors knew that even the scraps had magic. Our ancestors knew that nourishment from even the barest of pieces could feed the mind, body, and spirit. It's why I am not ashamed to be the descendant of slaves, of people who made a way out of no way. People who survived on hope and hopelessness. People who took parts of animals and vegetables that had no prior use and used them to nourish others. People who passed down those lessons to feed hundreds of thousands, who passed down those lessons to feed millions of Black folks. People who created a culture, an existence. It's why I am not ashamed to eat the foods that my ancestors ate. Every now and again I'll hear some bougie Black person condescendingly refer to some of the foods we eat—pigs' feet, chitterlings, grits—as "slave food." It's hard for people to accept the slave as anything more than the property they were. However, I see their humanity because I am them. We are the trauma they carried. We are their deaths. We are their joy and lives. We are their souls, and their food is our food.

There is no such thing as "better" food unless you think "better" meant what the slave masters ate. Why would I desire the food that fed my ancestors' abusers? The whole notion of food having soul is the removal of narrow standards. It was cooked from a place of love, necessary for the nourishment of those we love. My Black-ass grandmothers from the 1700s passed it down to my Black-ass grandmothers in the 1800s, who passed it down to my Black-ass grandmothers in the 1900s, who passed it to Big Nanny, who passed it on down to Lula Mae, who passed it down to Nanny. Nanny spent decades pouring herself into the food, and the food is an extension of her soul and the souls of every Black woman in our family before her. I just wish those other souls told her not to orange those damn yams that year.

I have such fond memories of all our Thanksgivings— especially the last one we got to spend with her. Eventually, we knew things would be different. Nanny's soul would eventually begin its transition to the other side. And that meant Grandma's hands had to become our hands.

Nanny passed away right after Thanksgiving of 2019. Although she was alive for the holiday that year, she wasn't really mobile or able to speak. But that morning, my mother and I went into her bedroom to tell her happy Thanksgiving. She was looking at us, and my mom said, "Garrett is gonna try to make your sweet potato pies." Nanny made a face and started shaking her head, and my mom and I laughed. Even though she was sick, parts of her spirit still came through strong. She knew Garrett had no business in anyone's kitchen.

Thanksgiving in 2019 was the first time we had to cook all the food. Using her recipes and doing the best that we could, we attempted our first Thanksgiving without our matriarch. Aunt Munch and I decided that we were going to tackle her mac and cheese. Aunt Sarah tried the yams— absent the orange flavoring. We did the best we could.

To be clear, the food was pretty good. It wasn't hers, but it was really tasty. Garrett was always the tester, and he gave us plenty of feedback. He told me and Aunt Munch to work on our "cheese ratio," because Nanny's dish always had so much cheese, but never enough to overwhelm you. Aunt Sarah did okay on the yams, but

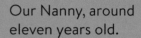

Our Nanny, around eleven years old.

Nanny, seated like the queen she was.

Rasul (left) and
Lil' Rall (right).

Nanny, Stephanie Elder
(my aunt Munch), and
Lil' Kevin.

Me and my younger
cousin Justice.

My brother, Garrett (left), and me (right)!

My brother, Garrett (left), and me, a little older, and our younger cousin Justice (front).

Lil' Rall (left), Rasul (right), and younger cousin CJ (front), ready for the wedding.

Uncle Rall with Lil' Rall—father and son.

Nanny and me at a Mount Zion AME Church function.

Lil' Rall (left) and Rasul (right), in the swing of their teen years.

Cousins photo! Cierra, Rasul, Garrett, me, and Lil' Rall (left to right).

Me, Lil' Rall, Rasul, Garrett, and, front and center, Gregory Johnson (my father).

Me and Kennedy.

Garrett (left) and Lil' Rall (right).

My aunt Crystal, Lil' Rall in uniform, Uncle Rall, and our proud Nanny.

A grand gathering! Aunt Sarah Elder, Uncle Rall, Kaye Johnson (my mother), and Aunt Munch (left to right) with Nanny.

Kennedy and me at my college graduation.

Nanny and me at the doctor, celebrating her one-year mark of fighting brain cancer.

they didn't get as soft as Nanny's and she still had to perfect that brown-sugar syrup sauce.

It was tough without her there. You could tell her presence was missing, but the spirit of that day was still full. She always knew her food was amazing, yet every Thanksgiving she would ask us, "How the food taste?" knowing we would give full rounds of applause and throw her roses and kisses from the audience. The kitchen was her home. Food was one of her many ways of showing love. Her love was in that food. Her spirit was in that food. Her soul was in that food.

Soul food is more than a style or type of cuisine. It is Black joy. It is the smile Garrett and I make when my mom fries chicken. The happiness in Rasul's face when he used to eat Nanny's yams. The hug Lil' Rall gave Nanny when he went vegetarian and she made special meals for him so he could partake with all of us. The big Christmas seafood feast tradition she started that had us feeling like we were on an episode of *Lifestyles of the Rich and Famous*. The food will always trigger the memories—the reminder that the soul never leaves us, even when the flesh is no longer here.

10

Wedding Bells and Brawls

Nannyism: "Once you put the trash on the
curb, you don't go back and get it."

It was 1997 and another typical summer in Jersey for
us, or at least we assumed it would be. Little did we
know, this summer would feature a heavyweight fight
between two family members that would be settled
some months later at a beautiful banquet hall.

Usually, June through August for me and Garrett
looked the same. For the first two weeks after school was
out, we would go to Nanny's house. For the next four,

we would rotate between camp—which we hated—in the mornings and Nanny's Lewis Avenue house in the evenings until my mother got off work.

A year earlier, Nanny threw us a curveball—she decided that our cousin Lil' Kevin should come and live with her. Although he was living with his mother, she wanted to make sure he wasn't running in the streets of Jersey City, and figured it would be good for him to be around family more often. That was Nanny, making sure we all had a chance in this world.

Lil' Kevin wasn't really little—he was tall and brown skinned and had a solid medium build. He lived in Jersey City with his mother and never had much of a relationship with his father, my uncle Kevin. I think there was some resentment there, especially considering the fact that Lil' Kevin was effeminate like me. Uncle Kevin always wanted a son more like Lil' Rall or Rasul. And even though Uncle Kevin loved his child, I don't think he ever processed having a son who was "different." Worse, Lil' Kevin grew up watching a father who adored me but couldn't show that same love to his son, who was just like me. Although Lil' Kevin was taken from us too soon (a moment I'll touch on later), we formed many good memories with him.

Anyhow, with Lil' Kevin in the picture, Lil' Rall and Rasul wanted to do something special that summer of 1997. They'd had a *long* year of fights in high school and were generally sick and tired of being in the small city of Plainfield every day. Realistically, there was nothing to do in our city aside from getting into trouble. And Lord knows they had their fair share of that. So, they came up with a plan....

The plan was for Lil' Rall, Rasul, and Lil' Kevin to spend the summer in Atlanta with Uncle Kevin. By this time, Uncle Kevin had been living in Georgia for more than five years and had done pretty well for himself. He had a beautiful home with a front and back yard and had worked his way up as a factory worker to make his own money—nothing like the Nanny-dependent thirty-plus-year-old he had been most of his life.

The boys' plan was also an attempt to reconcile the pretty nonexistent relationship between Uncle Kevin and Lil' Kevin. Uncle Kevin and Lil' Kevin didn't really see eye to eye and there were still years of hurt there, which Lil' Kevin rightfully deserved to feel. After all, the greater part of his rearing came from his mother and Nanny, not his father. They unfortunately never got the chance to reconcile, as Lil Kevin's life was cut short by a tragic event, with Uncle Kevin passing about five years later. I can only hope they did so in the afterlife.

Prior to this attempt at breaking out of Jersey, Lil' Rall, Rasul, and Lil' Kevin had never traveled without any adult supervision. Plus, the three of them clearly had a track record of fighting folks and carrying on, so the recipe for disaster was definitely there, especially if someone mixed the right ingredients. Instead of going to their parents, they went to the one and only Nanny to have this discussion. Although Nanny was the provider, disciplinarian, and caregiver, she was also practical and the person you needed on your side if you wanted to pull a stunt. If you made your case and it made sense, she would usually give you some leeway. This was also her method of giving you just enough rope to tangle yourself up.

They pleaded their case. Told her what bus they would be taking. Told her how much money each of them had saved to travel and how much they might need every few weeks in assistance. Told her what they would be doing every day while down in Georgia for the summer. Uncle Kevin had already agreed to let them stay, and everything was just waiting on Nanny's okay.

I think Nanny was proud that they didn't come to her with no bullshit. They came to her as young adults with everything lined up. She also probably thought a change of scenery would be good for them, considering that they seemed to stay in some mess in Plainfield. She agreed and told them she would talk with all their parents to *tell* them they were allowed to go. That next week Nanny bought three bus tickets and the boys took the fifteen-hour trip from New Jersey to Georgia. The three of them got there safely, and the family prayed hard that it would all work out...but, oh, how the prayers went unanswered. I don't know if God was napping or just ignoring us, but sometimes the best-laid plans go to absolute shit.

Everything was good for the first two days. But by day three, a combative spirit was building between Rasul and Uncle Kevin's new wife, Desiree. She never really took issue with Lil' Rall and Lil' Kevin, but for some reason, Rasul used to get under her skin. No matter what he did, she went off about it. Rasul left dishes in the sink, she was cussing at him. He was in the shower too long, she was cussing at him. There seemed to be nothing he could do right.

Truth be told, Rasul wasn't doing anything besides saying his piece back to her when she started with him, and even Uncle Kevin was on Rasul's side for most of the arguments. Of course, the boys were calling Nanny daily with the play-by-play. She was getting madder by the day, so much so that she wanted to go down there and bring them home, but they assured her they would be okay.

The final straw was the day Desiree intentionally locked them out of the house. To get back inside, Lil' Rall, Rasul, and Lil' Kevin had to wait for hours until Uncle Kevin got off work. Of course, by then, all three of them were ready to fight this woman. The argument that night got really bad, and my uncle Jeffrey, one of Old Daddy's nephews, came over.

As Desiree kept getting louder and louder—clearly drunk at the time—Uncle Jeffrey finally had enough and said, "Kevin, tell that bitch to shut the f*ck up!"

Uncle Kevin tried to play peacemaker, saying, "You ain't gotta call her all that, Jeffrey." At that point, everyone was pissed and arguing, so Uncle Jeffrey told the three boys to get their things and come with him.

For the rest of that summer they stayed at Uncle Jeffrey's house. They had no beef with Uncle Kevin, so he would come over to the house and visit them a few days out of the week, without his wife. The rest of the summer went off without an issue. However, Nanny was not going to let it go that easy.

That November, my uncle Brian—Uncle Jeffrey's brother—was getting married in New Jersey. Of course, Uncle Kevin was going to come, along with his wife, Desiree. It was a few days before the wedding, and the whole family was at Nanny's house. Uncle Kevin said he was going to come by to visit, and Nanny knew this was her chance to ask Desiree about the summer in Atlanta.

Of course, the family was talking about it before Uncle Kevin arrived. In the living room of Nanny's house sat my mother, Aunt Sarah, Garrett, and I, and some other family friends.

"I'm going to find out what she did to my grandsons,

and if she starts acting up, I'm-a knock her out," said Nanny.

"Mommy, be nice," said my mother.

"I'm-a be nice but I'm just saying."

Garrett had a grin on his face from ear to ear. Garrett was ready for the action to begin.

Now, mind you, if Nanny said she was going to knock someone out, then she was going to knock someone out—with either her words or her fists. Still, while there have been several fights over the years, the great thing about our family is that we've always been able to come back together. But that day, the hopes were that Nanny would behave.

A few minutes later, Uncle Kevin arrived. It was a great reunion, as we all hadn't seen him since he had moved to Georgia years before. But we all knew what Nanny was waiting for. After the hugs, we sat down in the living room and began with small talk before Nanny cut right to the chase.

"Where is this new wife at? I need to meet her," she said with her southern accent.

"Oh, she at the hotel room. She said she was tired from the ride up here. She will be at the wedding tomorrow."

Nanny sat back in her chair. "Oh, okay. Yeah, I can't wait to meet her and talk to her some."

And then Garrett, standing right next to Nanny, said it. "We gonna beat up your wife!"

Everyone's faces dropped.

Luckily Uncle Kevin took it as a joke and busted out laughing. "Man, Garrett. You crazy!"

"Garrett, cut it out," said Nanny as she gave him the look. Not the *I'm-a beat your ass* look, but the smirk saying, *You right, but keep it a secret.* We all started laughing and glancing at each other, breathing a sigh of relief and remembering why you couldn't just say things in front of Garrett unless you wanted everyone else to know about it, too. The visit was short, as Uncle Kevin needed to get back to his wife, but we knew what was brewing in the air.

The wedding and the ceremony went off perfectly. But of course, the kids were looking forward to the showdown. The reception, held in the hotel where we were all staying, was grand, and everyone danced all night. The speeches were beautiful, and the toss of the garter and bouquet were fun to watch, too. No expense was spared. However, an event so beautiful was about to turn into a fiasco.

Nanny sat at a table with my father, who by now was "drunk as a skunk." Even past that limit, he was still very much present and aware that the mission had not yet been completed. Although my dad was her son-in-law, they were only nine years apart and operated much more like the two heads of the family. Like two Black mob bosses of the Johnson-Elder gang.

"Well, the night is almost over, Lou. You gonna handle your business?" my father said to Nanny. Nanny looked at him and took a deep breath. She got up from the table and walked over to where Aunt Desiree was sitting. She pulled up a seat next to her, sat down, and said, "Hey, we need to talk about what happened this summer with you and my boys."

Desiree was "feeling no pain," as they would say, and likely one rung higher on the drunk scale than my father at this point. She turned to Nanny and said, "I don't need to talk to you about nothing, bitch."

A lady sitting at the table overheard her and said, "You don't talk to Mrs. Elder like that."

Desiree responded, "I talk to this bitch—" And then the words came to a stop.

Nanny swung back her big arm and unleashed a

backhand with the power of Mike Tyson. Aunt Desiree immediately fell to the floor, where she stayed. Nanny got up, straightened out her skirt with a quick brush-off, and walked back to the table to sit next to my father.

Luckily, most of the room didn't notice what happened, so the party continued. However, from the dance floor, Cierra (Aunt Crystal's daughter), Garrett, and I could see everything. Once Nanny sat back down, I walked over to the table and excitedly asked her, "What happened?"

She had a stern look on her face but said, "Nothing. Everything is fine," and then sat quietly.

My dad stated, "That's how we handle business."

Only five to ten minutes of the reception were left, so there was still a small chance that we could make it out without the whole event turning into an episode of *The Jerry Springer Show*. Unfortunately, that evening, the odds were not in our favor.

As the DJ wrapped up the party, people started to leave. Nanny was still sitting at her table near the exit to the hotel's main hallway and lobby. As Desiree, still intoxicated and enraged, walked past Nanny's table, she turned to her and said, "If you ever hit me again, I'll cut your throat." Within seconds, Aunt Crystal grabbed a champagne bottle and headed toward Desiree.

"Crystal, no!" my mother yelled, and grabbed her before she could swing.

By now, Uncle Kevin, also intoxicated, was yelling, "Who hit my wife? Who hit my wife?" under the assumption that one of the boys—Lil' Rall or Rasul—or his sisters had done it.

"Your *mother* hit your wife!" Uncle Rall yelled at him, but no one seemed to listen. My father sat at the table, watching everything.

By now, enough of the men at the party had dragged out my arguing uncles, and my aunts had exited with the rest of the wedding party. Everyone was now spilling out into the hallways and the lobby with lots of cursing and arguing and nervous guests. Trust and believe, some knew it was only a matter of time before the police arrived, so they got out of there as quickly as they could.

Garrett and I took the elevator with Nanny and a few other family members going to their rooms. When we exited on our floor, wedding guests were standing in the hallway arguing and yelling—but this time, the crowd included Rasul and Uncle Kevin going back and forth about what had happened in Atlanta. I had never seen Rasul so enraged.

Lil' Rall stood on the sidelines while Uncle tried to keep the peace, telling Uncle Kevin, "That's your fucking nephew. You really gonna fight your nephew?" By this time, the liquor was the driving force behind everything. The good thing was, Nanny didn't drink and was in control at all times. "Kevin, go to your hotel room! Rasul and Rall, go to your rooms, too. *Everyone*—go to your hotel rooms."

Just as quickly as the tempers rose, they all went down when everyone heard Nanny's voice. Everyone got really quiet, breathing hard and heavy with anger. However, we all listened to Nanny and went to our rooms for the evening. And like that, the night was done. Beautiful wedding. And a reception that turned into a beautiful nightmare with a bunch of mess to end the night. Although Nanny never got her answers, she got us all to some kind of resolution.

Years passed before we saw Uncle Kevin and Desiree

again. If my memory serves me correctly, the next time we saw them was 2007, when they came up for Lil' Kevin's funeral.

Leading up to the funeral, we weren't sure how it was going to go. Over the years, Nanny had spoken to Uncle Kevin on the phone, but she hadn't interacted with Desiree at all. By now, all the boys had forgiven Uncle Kevin, but they didn't have direct relationships with Desiree. While it seemed that the tensions had passed, you can never be sure what feelings may rise up once you see someone in person for the first time since an incident.

Nanny used to tell her children, grandchildren, nieces, and nephews all the time, once you put trash to the curb, you don't go back to get it. Meaning, when you are done with "it," whatever the "it" is, you don't let it back in your life. If you feel that thing is salvageable, then you do all the woulda, coulda, shouldas before you ever get to that point. Once you throw it all out, it's done.

Our family has had many situations where we have been wronged by others or wronged by a loved one to a point that we thought we could never come back from. Sometimes we need to step away from folks and situations because, in the moment, all we see is the rage. But we don't throw each other away, because once you do, that's it. There wasn't a gray area for Nanny when it came to this. Officially ending a relationship wasn't something she took lightly, and this situation was no different—that funeral was the time to make the decision whether this situation was worth fixing.

Happily, it all went well. Desiree was much kinder this time around. She still drank too much, but not to the point of becoming angry. She had good conversations with everyone, including Nanny. She was such a happy drinker, she did something that we still laugh and joke about to this day. At the house, there was fruit at the bottom of a sangria mix Aunt Sarah had made. Desiree had one taste of that fruit, and it was all she wanted to have all weekend. But she kept slurring her words and asking, "Is there any more of that *fute* back there?" We would laugh and get her more "fute."

This story was a valuable lesson for all of us. Even in the worst of times, our bonds could never be broken.

We fell out at a wedding and came back together for a funeral. Time truly heals all wounds, and we all just needed time. But even in the time apart, we stayed connected. We stayed family. And Aunt Sarah had another reason to remind Nanny, *"They put old people in jail!"*

She never listened.

11

Boyz to Men

Nannyism: "When you turn thirteen, it's the smell of fresh ass."

Teenagers.

It was around 1997 or 1998 that we were transitioning to adolescence, and that meant we were all going through that dreaded period of puberty. Things like biking and skipping rocks were no longer fun to us—now everything was about being cool. Seeing what the fashions were and matching them. Seeing what rappers and actors were doing and trying to live our lives following their every move.

We all went through the normal stages of puberty. It started with the facial hair, a small mustache starting to firm. Nanny would grab on your face and say, "Let me get a look at the dirt over your lip." Then the voices started to drop. We stopped sounding like little boys and started to talk much deeper. Then came the growth spurts—well, not for Lil' Rall and Rasul. They always stayed short. Between the ages of thirteen and fourteen, I shot up about five inches and was suddenly towering over both of them. Of course, other things started to happen biologically, as well. I had to have been only twelve or thirteen when I got my first pubic hair. I was so damn excited that I told Lil' Rall about it. He busted out laughing and gave me a high five. "You're becoming a man, Matt! Soon you'll be getting with girls." That's something we can both laugh at nowadays.

Puberty for Lil' Rall, Rasul, and Lil' Kevin meant girlfriends—girlfriends who took up their time away from me and Garrett, might I add. Rasul had one girlfriend for all four years while he was in high school. I can't recall her name, but I remember she was always really nice. Light skinned and short like Rasul. They were a happy little couple, and she was able to keep Rasul's crazy in check.

Lil' Rall had two girlfriends in high school, and the second one he really, really liked. Nanny didn't approve of her, though. But to be fair, Nanny didn't like anyone that they brought home. One time, Lil' Rall worked really hard to save up his money and buy his girlfriend a bracelet. Rall was romantic in that way, and he liked treating a girl really nicely. But Nanny just couldn't understand why he was spending so much money on a girl that "ain't all that." When it came to us, Nanny had some standards that seemed impossible, but ultimately she only wanted us to have people in our lives who cared and treated us as well as she did.

What I will say is that we never really *talked* about sex. Was I aware that Lil' Rall and Rasul were having sex? Yes, and I knew this because Aunt Crystal used to buy them condoms. She always felt it was better for them to protect themselves and not bring home any babies while they were still children themselves. But that was an unspoken truth. I remember being in high school or around boys who talked about sex often, but that was never our thing at home.

My personal puberty experience is a little different and a bit more graphic, but extremely important to tell. My story intersects with my cousin Lil' Kevin. Throughout the book I've mentioned how similar we were—effeminate. I grew up knowing I was different. Meaning, I liked girls and found them cute at times, but I knew I was physically attracted to boys. Lil' Kevin knew this, too, and I think he saw some of me in himself.

In my memoir *All Boys Aren't Blue* I go into details about the nonconsensual sexual encounters I had with my cousin Lil' Kevin. In that first book, I gave him an alias of "Thomas" because I wasn't ready to fully tell the story. Now I know the importance of telling it in its entirety. I can't repair something I never name. The encounters happened on two separate occasions when I was either twelve or thirteen and he was around eighteen. He used his influence and power over me to get me to perform oral sex on him. He also performed it on me.

Sexual assault and manipulation were my introduction into sexuality. From then on, puberty for me was trying to hide in plain sight. That experience with him changed my viewpoint on everything. One, it confirmed my arousal by men. Two, it put me in a place where I tried even harder to suppress the feelings that I was having. Made me suppress the memories of what happened and fall even deeper into a state of self-preservation, living as a shell of the person I truly was. I would go on to have crushes in high school, but those years forever changed me.

My family didn't know about what had happened between me and Lil' Kevin until many years later, and Nanny never knew about it. I remember when I wrote my first book, my aunt Sarah said, "Write your book and tell your truth. We will all be fine as a family." That is why, this time around, I decided to use his name and give his story the full truth—the good and the bad. Lil' Kevin was a great person who did some very wrong things, and that's important to say.

I would be almost twenty-one years old before I had consensual sex, and to this day, at thirty-four years of age, I've never had a boyfriend. In many ways I don't think I've fully worked through the things necessary to trust a person with that part of me, because of what happened in my teens. However, I didn't let it stop me from continuing to have other positive, memorable experiences.

Although there were difficult times, I can honestly say my teenage years were good. I ran varsity track in high school and was the captain of the varsity bowling team during my senior year. I had a few friends, too. Even though I sometimes stuck out as the effeminate one in my friend group, I could read folks for filth and some of the kids liked that. I got along with mostly everyone during those years. Instead of sex, I just focused on getting good grades, getting into college, and getting the hell out of New Jersey.

By the time Garrett was going through puberty, Lil' Rall, Rasul, and I had moved away and were starting our lives. I was in college when Garrett turned fifteen. Honestly, he had the best high school experience of us all. He had a girlfriend, he was popular, could play sports, and he was *still* the baby.

Although I wasn't nearby, I tried my best to support him as he navigated those teenage years. Garrett and I had only one conversation about his having sex for the first time, and it wasn't long. I had come home from college either my freshman or sophomore year and was driving him and his friends somewhere. While in the front passenger seat, he began to tell me this story about a girl coming over, and I could already tell where it was heading. I was about to say something, assuming his friends knew about the encounter—not realizing how low he was speaking—and he shushed me so his friends couldn't overhear us. I just looked over and nodded. And that was it.

The puberty years were very different for all four of us. What I will say is I truly believe we were fortunate to have so many women in our lives. When I think about how boys and young men are conditioned to be sexist and misogynistic—and, believe me, in many ways we unfortunately still were—our mentality wasn't so much about chasing girls (well, in my case, I wasn't concerned about finding *any* girl) or multiple sexual conquests as it was about finding that person who was good for us.

We live in a heteronormative society of double standards, and no double standard is more obvious than the conditioning of girls to do and be one thing, while we expect something else from boys—especially when it comes to sex. Men celebrate their son's "loss of virginity" but jump to kill someone else's son should he try to take their daughter's, never once concerned about the virginity their sons are "taking" from someone else's child. Additionally, sexual conquest for Black boys is often a rite of passage. Boys are conditioned to attain their manhood through sex. It's something we watch and imitate. Something we are taught.

Recently, there was an interview with the rapper Lil Boosie in which he publicly admitted paying for grown women and strippers to have sex with his son and nephews, all aged thirteen and younger. This is sexual assault and rape, yet it's behavior that has been publicly praised in the community. And, worse, who is protecting the young girls these parents are training their sons to conquer?

This cycle must end if we hope to see Black boys develop into strong men who aren't broken by societal standards. We should condition Black boys to respect those of the opposite gender without seeing rejection as a denial of their manhood and identity. Furthermore, straight Black boys and men should be conditioned to respect all identities, with the understanding that their Blackness is no different from the Queer and trans person's Blackness. Lil' Rall, Rasul, Garrett, and I were fortunate to have the women of our family—Black women who taught us how to treat Black folks across the board.

During those teenage years, Garrett and I were lucky enough to be preteens with all-the-way teens, which meant that anything Lil' Rall and Rasul were doing, we also did. If they were sneaking and drinking liquor out the cabinet, so were we. If they were sneaking out of the house, so were we. And if they were getting into altercations, we were right there, too.

Another favorite story of ours is the day we took the car and went for a joyride around town. Lil' Rall had finally gotten his license, after the third attempt, so now our favorite babysitter was able to assist the adults.

"Can you pick Matt and Garrett up from school?"

"Can you run to the grocery store and pick up some sugar?"

Despite the constant errands, getting the keys to the

car was always something we had dreamed about, and finally one of us had reached that age.

The car, however, was *not* some prized possession. In addition to the station wagon, Nanny purchased the ugliest brown minivan I had ever seen in my life. This was before the era of oval-shaped minivans. It was like driving in an oversized Chinese food box container with wheels. You couldn't speed in it because it struggled to get over sixty miles per hour. You couldn't look cool in it because…it was a mess.

That day of the joyride, Lil' Rall was simply supposed to pick us up from school and bring us back to Nanny's house. After picking up Garrett from elementary school, Rall pulled up to meet me at the middle school. "Hurry up, Matt," he said. "We gotta roll out."

Now, this usually meant a fight was about to happen, with either him or Rasul. I hopped in the van with eighteen-year-old Rall driving, nine-year-old Garrett strapped in the front seat, and sixteen-year-old Rasul crouched in the back. Lil' Rall rode us around town, looking for this boy that Rasul was supposed to fight at the high school that day who went ghost. We were driving up the street when they saw him, a boy named

Kelly, walking with his friends. This next image was like a scene from a movie. Rasul slid that minivan door open while Lil' Rall was still driving. Just as the van passed the group of boys, Lil' Rall slowed and Rasul jumped out like he was Wesley Snipes in *Blade*.

"You was talking all that shit today—square up, nigga!" Rasul shouted.

We *all* hopped out of the car at this point. There were a few boys with them, so we had to make sure no one tried to jump Rasul. Everyone stood back so that Rasul and Kelly could "shoot the fair one," or fight each other without interference from anyone else.

Rasul and Lil' Rall were also trained boxers. Their father, Uncle, was a Golden Gloves boxing champ as a young adult. He made the newspaper and everything. Although I never got involved in boxing, whenever we had some free time together, Uncle would put me in gloves and teach me how to fight.

Rasul ducked as Kelly swung and missed. Rasul connected twice and kept weaving and bobbing as Kelly, who was bigger than him, tried to swing. In one move, Kelly lunged forward, while Rasul took a step back. Kelly missed Rasul again, but when Rasul backtracked, he stumbled over a tree stump coming out of the ground and fell. I thought Kelly would use that as a chance to get on top of him; instead, he and his friends took off running.

Rasul was pissed. His fighting prowess meant something to him, so the fact that he wasn't able to get Kelly like he wanted to sat on his mind for a while. However, we all were proud of him. We saw it for what it was— another story we could reminisce about one day.

Decades later, we talked about this moment, and Rasul remembered it as a loss. As Rasul retold the story to me, Garrett, and Lil' Rall, Lil' Rall looked at him and said, "You didn't lose that fight."

"You tripped over the tree stump or the uneven curb," Garrett chimed in, "but Kelly never hit you."

"Rasul," I said, "do you really not remember that as a fight you won?"

It's like they say when people are arguing—there is your truth, their truth, and somewhere in the middle is the *real* truth. No matter how we each remember those times, the stories are still valid and vivid. Different viewpoints but a shared truth that can't be erased. We do our best to allow grace to get things wrong and make mistakes. Even in our wrongs, we still had each other's backs.

Our teenage years held many more great, messy moments. There was the night when Lil' Rall was in charge and we raided the liquor cabinet in the house, thinking everyone was gone for the night. When Nanny and Aunt Sarah got home early, drunken sixteen-year-old Rasul ran and hid under the dining room table, while Garrett and I giggled and faked our way through it and Lil' Rall handled the explaining. I can't help but laugh as I write this. Our shared truth was a lie, but the joy we had that night was the absolute truth, regardless.

Society often tells only one side of the Black story, more often than not because it's not being written by us. Even when we are allowed to write it, it often has to use our trauma as the catalyst for the storytelling. However, I have no desire to tell our story without the joy and magic we created with one another. We were Black boys becoming young adults. Still growing, messing up, and never losing the love of just being in each other's presence.

My healing, in regard to my experiences with Lil' Kevin, doesn't negate the fact that what happened to me was wrong.

I don't believe that you can hold anyone who has passed away "accountable." However, it's still important to name what one has done to help those who are still dealing with these types of situations in the living. Abusers need to be held accountable. The abused deserve healing and restoration. I don't believe in punishment as justice. I truly believe in restoration for all involved.

12

All Good Things Must Come to an End

Nannyism: "It ain't harmony if all y'all singing the same note. The harmony is in the difference."

Sometimes, the people who once were the central parts of our lives leave and others appear to fill those voids. That describes our thoughts about Lil' Kevin—he was the cousin that came to visit us a few times a year and soon became part of our daily life.

Lil' Kevin was the life of the party. Growing up in the projects in Jersey City for most of his adolescence, Kevin didn't always have it easy. He was often fighting, especially because many assumed he was gay and would hurl slurs at him in an attempt to bully him. However, this got a lot of people's asses whooped, as Lil' Kevin was easily six feet two, and although not muscular, he was solid with a medium frame.

In 1996, after getting into a fight and potentially facing prison, Kevin came to live with us in Plainfield. I can recall Nanny saying to him when he arrived, "You know what kind of bird doesn't fly? A jailbird." His jaw dropped as she read him for filth. We all knew he needed to get out of Jersey City or it was going to be the death of him.

Lil' Rall and Rasul liked having Kevin around because he reminded them of their early days. Also, the three of them were completely nuts. They would take on anyone of any size and did not care about the consequences.

Lil' Rall was working at Toys R Us around the time Kevin moved in. He usually worked in the video game section but would sometimes help cut up boxes in the loading dock area. From time to time, he would bring box cutters home for Rasul, Lil' Kevin, and himself. Lil' Kevin showed them how to use the box cutters in a fight and they would walk around with them all the time, hiding them in their Timberland boots. As I said...they were absolutely nuts, and I have to laugh out loud at what we were doing back then.

Together, we were a mini-gang of five boys. Nanny really instilled in us a mantra of brotherhood. She didn't care who started the argument—'cause she would whoop everyone anyway—but she cared that, in the end, we all had made up. She knew we would need one another and during those times, we depended on each other hard.

Although the five of us (our usual group, plus Kevin now) usually saw one another at Nanny's, we all had our separate lives and didn't spend as much time together. However, one night during the winter of 1997, Lil' Kevin just *had* to go to the local skating rink, Skate 22. The rink was about twenty-five minutes from my parents' house, and on Thursdays and Fridays, they would host Teen Night. On one hand, Teen Night meant you could have fun and socialize with people your age. On the other hand, these nights also brought *a lot* of weekly fighting, as you had teens coming from predominantly rival Black high schools all over the county. It was the perfect recipe for a complete disaster. Somehow, Lil' Kevin managed to rally the rest of us to come with him.

Lil' Kevin asked my mother if she could drop us off and pick us up. She was reluctant, as was my father (since he was a cop and knew how many fights at the skating rink made the news). But she agreed, as long as we all went together. Lil' Rall, Rasul, and Lil' Kevin wanted me to go with them, too, and my mother allowed it. At the age of twelve, I was taller than Lil' Rall and Rasul, so there would be no questioning if I was a teenager, and they rarely checked IDs. Poor Garrett was only ten at the time and too young to go, so he spent the night at a friend's house.

Around seven that night, my mother picked up the four of us and drove us out to Skate 22 for our first Teen Night. Of course, Lil' Rall, Rasul, and Lil' Kevin had no intention of actually skating. Skate 22 had a dance floor, food court, and arcade, so they were going to use the time to hit on girls. I, on the other hand, was going to Rollerblade.

We all waited in line, paid for our entry, got our wristbands, and made it inside. Instead of using a locker, I just put my sneakers near Lil' Rall and Rasul, who decided to post up at the food court. Earlier that day, Lil' Rall told a girl he would be there, so he was waiting on her and keeping an eye on me the whole night. Lil' Kevin decided he wanted to dance, so he stayed on the dance floor. I wanted to skate, so I stayed in the center rink. The main thing was, we all decided to be on our best behavior.

Everything went pretty well for the first two hours. Lil' Rall even skated with me for a few minutes so I wouldn't feel alone out there. Things were good... until Lil' Kevin walked over from the dance floor to the food court area.

"This dude over there keeps bumping me and looking at me while I'm dancing!"

Lil' Kevin could dance well. However, the way that he used to dance would probably be described today as flamboyant. That is to say, there was always this underlying assumption of Lil' Kevin's sexuality. It wasn't just the dancing, though. Like me, his mannerisms could be described as effeminate—the way he was soft-spoken and had a little bit of sass in his reactions. One of the main reasons Kevin stayed in fights was because kids and even adults teased him about his possibly being gay.

"Look, Kevin," Lil' Rall responded, "we are *not* here for that tonight. Just let it go."

Lil' Kevin went back to dancing, but Lil' Rall and Rasul already knew they would need to keep an eye out for him the rest of the evening. About twenty minutes later, Lil' Kevin came back and said the boy was *still* doing it.

"Kevin," Lil' Rall told him, "just let it go. We'll leave in a few anyway, it's not that serious." By this point, we were getting closer to the end of the night and we knew my mother would be arriving soon.

As the rink began making the closing announcements, you could see a commotion on the dance floor. Rall and Rasul looked from across the room to try and grasp what was happening.

"Oh, shit," Rasul said. "That's Kevin!" He immediately grabbed me from the rink and told me to put my sneakers on. Lil' Rall ran over to Lil' Kevin, who was now being dragged into the front foyer section by a security guard. Kids were now rushing outside in a stampede. Lil' Rall was within talking distance of the security guard who had Lil' Kevin pinned on a wall, while kids flooded the parking lot. This security guard was significantly bigger than Lil' Kevin.

"Hey, that's my cousin!" Lil' Rall yelled. "Get off him!"

"Fuck this faggot," the security guard yelled back.

Lil' Rall cocked back and punched the security guard in the face.

By this point, another security guard came up and started fighting with Lil' Rall. Mind you, kids were still running out of the building. The security guard began choking Lil' Rall, even while Lil' Rall was still swinging on him, and Lil' Kevin was in a full-on fistfight with the other one. By this time, Rasul and I finally made it to the foyer to see everything. Rasul, box cutter in hand, slashed the arm of the guard who was choking his brother.

The security guard fighting Lil' Kevin turned on Rasul. But before he could grab him, I swung my Rollerblade and connected right with his face. This gave us just enough time to escape to the parking lot. In the distance, we saw my mother's car. The four of us took off running, opened the doors, and jumped in.

"They fighting—let's get out of here!"

As she pulled off, she said, "This is why I ain't want y'all to come here. These kids don't know how to act."

With the imminent danger gone, we all sat in the car on the ride home, laughing at each other, knowing the whole time we *were* the fight that night.

When we used to get into fights with one another, it was because we weren't in tune. We were all trying so hard to be right or "one-up" one another that we lacked harmony. But when we came together, we were unstoppable. "It ain't harmony if all y'all singing the same note," Nanny used to say. "The harmony is in the difference." Her words reminded us that our differences connected us and brought us in tune. And when we all figured out how to work together, we could move as a unit of love and protection for one another. In many ways, that fight was our last hoorah, as we knew the dynamics of our lives would soon change.

A few weeks later, Lil' Rall, now eighteen, officially headed off to the Air Force. Our fearless leader was taking his next step toward adulthood. No more babysitting of the little cousins. No more joyrides and street brawls. No more sneaking liquor and playing cards all night. Now we had to learn life without each other in our daily existence.

The year 1998 was a time of change for the entire family. That summer, Uncle and Aunt Crystal decided to move from New Jersey to Virginia. At first it was very hard on us. With Lil' Rall gone, there would be no more barbershop weekends or getting hot wings with Aunt Crystal. Rasul didn't want to move to Virginia and decided to stay with our great-grandmother, who lived in Bayonne, New Jersey, a city thirty minutes from Plainfield. This meant that we would see less and less of him, too, as he approached the age of eighteen and considered what he wanted to do with his life.

Lil' Kevin stayed around long enough to graduate from high school. Afterward, he decided to move back to Jersey City with his mother and the other side of his family. We would see him from time to time at family cookouts and certain family events. He was a sweetheart but was always fighting someone, and never quite got his life on track.

Unfortunately, Lil' Kevin's life was cut short at the age of twenty-six, while defending one of our cousins in Jersey City. Lil' Kevin was at a party with our cousin Amy, who had gotten into an altercation with a group of men. Although Kevin didn't originally come to the party with her, he saw what was happening and decided to walk her out. Once they got outside, the argument continued and escalated to a fight between Kevin and each of the men, one on one.

There were three of them, but they decided to fight Kevin individually. Kevin beat up the first one. Then he beat up the second. By this time, Kevin was openly gay, and the men, stuck on trying to prove their masculinity, were embarrassed that they were getting beat up by a gay man. Still, the third man decided to fight Kevin. In the middle of the fight, the man pulled out a gun and shot Lil' Kevin in the head.

It was tough on the family. Nanny lost a grandchild. Uncle Kevin lost his son. My mom and aunts and uncles lost a nephew. Our group of five lost one of the vital parts of our crew. Like anything else, only time heals all wounds. Despite the complicated relationship Lil' Kevin and I had, my love for him as my cousin never stopped. He was a Black gay boy who experienced the same harms and violences as I did. For me, his mistakes, flaws, harms, and abuses didn't outweigh the fact that he was my family and no one had the right to take him away from us.

It would be years before the original four of us reunited. We weren't estranged, but as we got older, our relationships continued to change.

Throughout the years, Garrett and I were always together. We even went to Virginia Union University together—I was a senior while Garrett was a freshman. But after college, I stayed in Virginia and made my home there for nearly ten years. Garrett came back to Plainfield right after graduating so that he and the youngest grandchild, Kennedy, could forever fight over who was Nanny's favorite.

Rasul hopped around a lot like a nomad, but that was always the spirit of Rasul—never one to let roots build up under his feet. He held a lot of hurt that often kept him away, though there were moments when he would visit Uncle and Aunt Crystal or come see Nanny and the aunts or even visit me. He and Lil' Rall maintain their love–hate–love relationship, but one day time will heal this wound, too. Lil' Rall left the Air Force and had a few ups and downs, but certainly lives life on the up and up now.

Our harmony is in our differences, and no matter what, taking care of one another is in our DNA. It's what Nanny taught us and a rule by which we continue to live our lives. And, Lord knows, we needed every lesson as we entered the final chapter with our matriarch and queen.

13

Amazing Grace

Nannyism: "You can't worry and pray. You either worry about it or pray about it. But once you leave it in God's hands, it's in God's hands."

Nearer, my God, to thee. Nearer to thee. E'en though it be the cross that raiseth meeeee!

I can still hear Nanny's voice singing that song. That damn "Nearer, My God, to Thee" was one of her favorite hymns, and she sang it with all of her spirit. Although when Nanny sang it, she always said the wrong words.

"Nero" was the word she used, and she used to sing it so loudly in the pew, almost daring someone to challenge her.

Nanny took great pride in going to church every Sunday. She raised us all as African Methodist Episcopalians, a doctrine started by Richard Allen, a former slave from Philadelphia. In 1787 Richard Allen founded the African Methodist Episcopal Church, which was the first independent Black denomination in the United States. As a minister, educator, and writer, he was an incredibly active and influential Black leader in early America, and his work lives on. Mount Zion AME Church in Plainfield, New Jersey, would be our church home for many years.

Nanny used to make us take part in *every* church function until we were old enough to decide whether we wanted to attend every Sunday or not. At young ages, Nanny enlisted us in the Angels of Zion choir. Lil' Rall, Rasul, Garrett, and I were required to go to choir rehearsal every Wednesday and learn songs with other children. Being the superstar in his head that he was, Rasul was a soloist and would put on performances in the church as if he were James Brown. The reverend, deacons, and church members ate up every moment of it. Choir was the one place that Rasul felt like he was the center of attention. His spirit was always the strongest of the four of us. He was always so free with reckless abandon. So what if the tree was ten feet in the air? He was going to be the one to jump down from it. And in church he was a star. I can't even lie, that was the one thing I was jealous of—Rasul didn't fear anything.

Lil' Rall was fine with taking a backseat at church. We'd stand in the choir together, the two of us singing off-key with the rest of the kids in white robes. Nanny sat in her normal section with my mom and her church friends, wearing a big hat to match her big diamonds and her coordinated church outfit.

When Garrett and I were preteens, we also joined the church's liturgical dance team. There was certainly a belief that liturgical dance should be for girls only, and Garrett eventually left the dance group because it challenged his "Tuffy" moniker. But I stayed because it put me in touch with my effeminate side—it was a chance to be myself. I could tell it made folks uncomfortable, but I'm grateful to Aunt Sarah, who ran the squad. I'm sure she saw the looks and heard the whispers, but she let me be me. She let a boy be different.

As we all got older, our relationship with church began to change, but Nanny had already instilled in us that faith and trust in the Lord. Although I eventually stopped attending Sunday services, I often participated in special productions put on by the church, such as plays and musicals. Our greatest feat was starting the soup kitchen, where Nanny and I would make dinner and deliver it to sick and shut-in church members every week. The Black church for many isn't just about biblical lessons but rather a larger piece of the Black experience and a way of life for generations over.

The Christian church is the foundation of religion for many Black people in this country, and its roots are intertwined with our enslavement here—with many of those principles pulled from white religion. Our first churches predate the ending of enslavement, so our relationship with God is tied to our trauma—and, often, the faith and hope we need either to escape that trauma or fight it.

Many of our Black-led organizations, such as the

NAACP or Black Greek-Letter Organizations, are based on Christian principles. These principles often uphold homophobia, misogyny, sexism, and patriarchal ideologies. Although the church has been a place of worship and salvation for many, it has been a center of pain for many others. There are numerous discussions nowadays about younger Black people leaving traditional Baptist and AME church settings and opting for religions and teachings that are more worldly and spiritual—a sign of the times, as many of us are starting to understand the damage that white supremacy and patriarchy have inflicted on our community, and how the Black church can play a role in upholding traditions that go against the younger generation's views on life.

My relationship with the Black church has never been easy. Knowing from a young age that I was Queer, I learned very quickly that the church wasn't always the safest place to express myself. One of my most traumatic moments with religion occurred when I was in my early twenties. I went to a pastor looking for advice on being gay and he told me, "I can't accept you as you are." That was the last time I was a member of anyone's church.

However, the four of us boys are all still Christians.

We believe in the power of prayer, although none of us attend regular services. I'm much more spiritual now and in tune with my ancestors and my connection to the universe, while Lil' Rall, Rasul, and Garrett still opt for tradition. Whatever our beliefs, we support one another. And no matter who we each pray to, we all pray for each other.

Nothing could ever break Nanny's faith. She still believed that God had all the answers and made no mistakes. Every night, she prayed hard for us, and with every win or victory, the first thing out her mouth was, "Hallelujah!" followed by, "Thank you, Lord!"

As a Black woman she often gave more to others than to herself; I can surmise that God had to be her place of refuge. Black grandmothers—Black women in general—are asked to pour so much into a world that never seems to fill them up. She was the matriarch, not just to her immediate family but to all the family. You need advice? Call Aunt Lou. You need a loan? Call Louise or Nanny or Mommy. Someone gotta get put in check? Get Big Lou on the phone. When others in the family dropped the ball, she was the one to pick it up.

But not even the Lord could prepare any of us for this next part. Although she taught us that we should never question God and why he does the things that he does, I'm still left with more questions than answers, and answers I will probably never get. Knowing that death is a part of life doesn't stop the fact that it's one of the hardest things to cope with.

Brain cancer was the diagnosis the doctors stated in July 2018. Lil' Rall, then thirty-eight; Garrett, then twenty-nine; and I, then thirty-two; were right there for the first surgery; and I wouldn't have it any other way. We sat together in that waiting room. Me, the emotional one on the verge of tears. Garrett, stoic and holding it in. And Lil' Rall, making sure the two of us were okay.

"You need something to eat, Matt? Garrett, you good?" he'd say.

Unfortunately, Rasul had become a bit estranged. Though I hadn't talked to him in a while, I still sent him a message that Nanny was having surgery and updated him when it was over. No matter how far apart we may have been, we knew that she would've wanted us to keep one another close.

Nanny survived that first brain surgery. The ongoing diagnosis was grim, but we decided to fight by her side. For a year, Nanny fought through chemotherapy and radiation treatments. We breathed a sigh of relief at each appointment when there was a positive update from the doctor. It meant we had more time. Time to be with her. Time to keep making memories. But we knew one of those appointments was going to be the one when she wouldn't get the good news.

During that first year, though, she made sure to check one important thing off her list. In the AME church, you have a christening ceremony—it's when you turn over your life to Christ and live in those Christian teachings. All of Nanny's children and grandchildren were christened, most of us at Mount Zion AME Church. Nanny was the last living great-grandparent for the newest addition to the family, Garrett's first child, who we affectionately call Baby G. Nanny knew she had to see Baby G get christened. In January 2019, dripping in her diamonds and wearing her full-length mink coat and hat, she sat front and center as Baby G's life was turned over to the Lord in front of a packed Mount Zion AME Church, the same church we had all come through before. The grin on her face that day was something that none of us will ever forget. She was smiling ear to ear and thankful to the Lord for being able to see another milestone, especially one so deeply tied to her faith. From that moment, she even started talking about things she'd do when she turned eighty, which would have been two years down the line. She was fighting to live.

Nanny's MRI appointments were every other month, and I was still living in Brooklyn, so I traveled to Jersey to make every appointment. We would take a picture with each good diagnosis and post them online. The world was now on this journey with us.

In July 2019, I decided to move back home to Plainfield with my parents—a story that could be its own book—because I had a gut feeling I was going to be needed. Nanny was still doing well with treatment, but something just didn't feel right. A Nannyism of hers kept popping up in my thoughts: *You may have to wipe my ass someday.* Meaning, there would come a day when we would have to fully take care of her, and we shouldn't fear her death but instead help her with the transition. Three weeks later, Nanny's brain tumor returned.

Once again, she went into battle. Another brain surgery, but this time things were much different. We had to wait three weeks before they would operate, but that first week she stayed in the hospital. And who should show up to surprise her? None other than Rasul Elder himself! My mom and I sat with him in the hospital, and he brought his daughter with him so that she could visit Nanny, too.

Rasul's appearance had changed a lot over the years. He was still light skinned and thin, but much shorter than me now. He had a bald head with dreads around the outside. Even though it had been years since Nanny had seen him, he still wanted to get some things off his chest. My mom and I looked at each other, knowing this could go right and be fine, or it could go left and I would have to fight him in the hospital. Luckily, it went right.

Rasul still held a lot of angst from our childhood. Although he had many fond memories, he often felt that everyone took Lil' Rall's side over his and that he was gravely misunderstood. He harbored unsettling feelings about his parents and Nanny's decisions in raising us. But Nanny said one thing that calmed him: "I did the best I could with what I had. No matter what, I always loved you." I think he knew this, but sometimes you just need to hear the words. I know that a part of him was healed that day.

Rasul and I have had many ups and downs over the years—sometimes more downs than ups. It took years of talking and learning from each other to reach the beautiful place we're at now. But that visit at the hospital was both necessary and healing. It felt good to have him back around, and I knew that it made Nanny happy to know her boys were going to be all right.

Still, Nanny's strong recovery after the first surgery just didn't seem to be happening this time around. With each visit to the rehab facility, you could see her doctors' faces gently trying to tell us that this might be her last round. When we finally left rehab the week before her next appointment, people clapped for her. But I think everyone knew. The doctors. The nurses. We all knew.

Nanny was also very intuitive with her body and she realized something wasn't right with the recovery.

While my mother and aunts went out of town for a few days, I stayed with her at her house in Plainfield to "Nannysit." Two days before her next appointment, she and I sat in her bedroom.

"Matt," she said, "can I tell you something?"

I already knew what was coming next. She had been talking to God lately, and I could tell she knew her marching orders, but needed to get them off her mind and her chest.

"Yeah, what's going on?"

She sat up in the bed and said, "I don't have too many long days left."

"You really feel that?"

"Yeah. But I've made peace with this, and I know God is gonna take care of y'all."

Two days later at the hospital, her doctors told us there was nothing they could do, as the tumor had returned for the third time. We sat in that room—Nanny, my mom, Uncle Rall, Aunt Sarah, and me. Tears started rolling and she told us all in that voice, "Stop crying." She reiterated that God was in control and she wouldn't let this break her faith. She always said she didn't want to die in a hospital, so we brought her back to her home.

The first weeks were steady, but we noticed small things. Her speech started to slur. She would say, "Hand me the watch," or "Hand me the soap," when she really meant the remote. We would give her food to eat with her medicine, and she would question how many pills we gave her. She would try to eat with a fork holding it backward. It got so bad that eventually she started eating everything with her hands.

Week to week, we watched her condition worsen, from being able to move around to being unable to walk without help. Each day we noticed a new symptom of confusion. Then came the loss of appetite and the refusal to take any more medicine. Finally, she went from full sentences to a few words to no words at all.

One night after my mother and I had gotten Nanny down to sleep, we got a call at about three AM from Aunt Toni, who was watching her for the night: *Auntie fell out of bed.* My mother and I headed to her house, which was only about seven minutes away from us. When we went upstairs, she was lying with her legs in the bed and her body in a lounge chair that we positioned by the bed to prevent her from falling to the ground. The first thing I did was move her from the chair to the floor so I could help her rise.

"You have to stand, Nanny," I said, but I realized she couldn't. I looked at my mother and said aloud, "I don't think she can move her legs anymore." By this point Nanny was almost nonverbal and couldn't tell us one way or the other. So I used everything in me to pick her up and roll her into her bed. We tucked her in tight. That was the last day she ever walked.

Those next two weeks we did everything for her. We washed her, changed her, and gave her water as she slowly stopped eating and lost her ability to move anything but her arms. We played Aretha Franklin's *Amazing Grace* album on repeat. It was her favorite, with a lot of her beloved gospel songs, including the title track. We were there to make certain she left the physical world with all the grace and care she had given others her entire life.

The Monday before Thanksgiving, her new hospice nurse arrived. She checked Nanny's blood pressure and did all the normal tests, and said she was okay. I stopped the nurse before she left and said, "We keep putting socks on her feet, but they seem to stay cold."

The nurse took a deep sigh and put another pair of gloves on. She took off Nanny's socks and she saw purple dots forming on her feet. She turned to me and said, "She is starting to transition and at a minimum has four days left."

"Mommy," I yelled. "You need to get up here!"

My mom, not suspecting anything, came upstairs and walked around to the head of Nanny's bed.

"Mommy," I repeated, "she said she is starting to transition."

My mom looked at the nurse, who confirmed, "She will pass in as little as four days."

"Four days?" my mom responded. "From now?"

"Yes."

My mother sat on the bed next to Nanny and started rubbing her head, telling her it was going to be okay. By this point, Nanny wasn't really responsive, but we could feel she knew what was going on.

That day, my mother and I decided to transport Nanny from her house to live with me and my parents. Garrett came over and the two of us helped the hospice team carry her into the ambulance before driving across town to my parents' home. This move was important—for years, Grandma Lula Mae, Nanny's mother, stayed in the same bedroom that my Nanny was in. Grandma Lula Mae had had a heart attack in that house and passed away during transport to the hospital. We knew Nanny didn't want her final days to be in that house and we guaranteed that they wouldn't be.

Once we transported her inside, we moved her to the old bedroom Garrett and I used to share. We got her in the bed and told her, "We got you out of your sister's house." We all started clapping. She lifted her left arm in the air and softly said, "Amen. Amen. Amen."

Nanny lived in the house with us for a week, once again defying the odds and making it one day longer than expected. On the morning of December 3, she took her last breath. The day to lay her burdens down had finally come. She got to experience a freedom unlike any other—not death, but her next form of life. To take up space in a place where cancer could no longer harm her. The ancestral place.

Although I had just turned thirty-four years old a few weeks prior, I might as well have been eight or eighteen all over again. I felt like a lost child. All of us felt like lost children. They say grief is having a lot of love with no place to put it. The only reason we were able to get through it was because we decided to put that love into one another.

We decided that Nanny had to go out in grand fashion, like the royalty she was. Much like when a celebrity or a high-up state official passes, she deserved to be adored by the city where she had planted roots for so many decades. A horse-drawn carriage ride throughout the city. Her casket sitting in a beautiful carriage with glass windows and her name NANNY inscribed. It was going to be glorious.

Her funeral date was set for December 14. Lil' Rall and Rasul got to town the day before. It had easily been more than a decade since the four of us had been together. We always kept in contact, but usually three of us would meet in one place, with one of us missing. But now her four boys were back together and ready to take on the hardest thing any of us would ever have to do. And we were going to let her go in the place where it all started for us: Mount Zion AME Church.

The night of the wake, we all held it together pretty

well. There were a few tears here and there, but Lil'
Rall, Rasul, Garrett, and I honestly consoled others more than ourselves. My mom sang "Because You
Loved Me" by Celine Dion, which was the part that
broke us all. My mom, Nanny's oldest child, who had
been one of her main caregivers at the end, sang her
own mother home.

That next day was the funeral. In many ways, we
wished Nanny could have seen it. And in many ways,
we also knew she *did* see all of it. We loaded up in two
limousines—children in the first car and grandchildren
in the second. The horses began pulling her carriage
through the city with a full police escort, as if we were
burying royalty. People came out of their houses to
wave. As we pulled up to the church, we had a bag-
piper playing "Amazing Grace." The grandchildren
lined up and we got her casket out of the hearse. They
brought her to the front of Mount Zion and began the
processional.

My brothers and I stood at the front as people came
in to say their final goodbyes. When it was almost
time to close the casket, the four of us decided to go
up together. We held one another as tears rolled down

our faces. I thanked her for raising us like she did. Then it was finally time for us to let her go. We took our seats and went through the service. As family members shared their memories of Nanny, their words convinced me that our family would make it through. Our baby cousin, and the only granddaughter, Kennedy, wrote a beautiful speech.

Dear Nanny,

You already know who this is, so I won't have to say my name again.

You were the very first best friend I had, before I knew what it meant to have a best friend. You were the perfect example of what any grandmother should be. You always loved everyone around you, and you had one of the best personalities in the whole world. Nanny, although you're not down here, I'll never forget all the great times we shared. Like the time you chipped your dentures when we ate chicken, so we drove all the way to Jersey City to get them fixed. Or all the adventures we went on when you could drive. I'm going to miss those days when you used to drive me to school in your nightgown and winter coat, while we listened to "Clean Up Woman" by Betty Wright.

You were always proud of me. Anytime you felt someone was doing me wrong, you never hesitated to stand up for me. Even if

I couldn't be with you every day as I got older, I always thought about you. I just want to say that, Nanny, you're the light in my world and you'll continue to be the light in my world. Even though it's sad, I know that you're finally at peace.

Love you for eternity.

Sincerely,
Kennedy (your favorite grandchild)

About twenty minutes later, after Garrett read his own speech at her funeral, he grabbed the mic and said, "And, for the record, I'm still her favorite grandchild!" The whole church erupted in laughter. Even at her funeral, we were still having that argument like nothing had changed. It would have been easy for us to fall apart after losing a person so powerful. A spirit so full of life and energy and wisdom. But we know that falling apart would be a disrespect to all the gifts and talents and love she told us to share with the world.

Soon after, Uncle spoke, and there was a line in there that I'll never forget: "You can't outchurch my mother. No one in here could ever outchurch my mother."

He was right. Nanny was a shit-talking, old-school southern Black woman from Spartanburg, South Carolina. She was a five-time survivor of cancer until her sixth battle took her home. Even in the end, when she could barely speak, one of the last words she was able to form was "amen." Nanny loved the Lord, and she raised us to be the same way.

To cite writer Brooke Obie, there is a test of how we must handle Black art. The Walker–Hurston test, as she puts it, draws from an Alice Walker quote in the introduction of the great Zora Neale Hurston's post-humous work *Barracoon*, and I use it to guide all my work. *"Those who love us never leave us alone with our grief. At the moment they show us our wound, they reveal they have the medicine."*

Nanny's story is Black art, and my intention is to never leave us at the point of grief and hurt. If I'm taking you to that place, then I better damn well be doing the work to pull you through it and pull you out of it. I'm sad that my grandmother is no longer here in the physical world, but the physical is the only thing that has changed. When we want to pray with her, we pray with her. When we want to talk to her, we talk to her. We ask for her guidance and look to the signs she leaves us. When I have a dream about her and she comes through as clear as day, I wake up and smile as a tear of joy rolls down my face. What a blessing it is, indeed, to know I have the powerful spirit of Nanny in my life.

Nanny, the most rewarding thing I've ever done in my life was stay right by your side, preparing you to be an ancestor. I wasn't watching your journey toward death—I was witnessing your journey toward peace from an Earth that has always been intent on harming you as a Black woman, harming us as Black people. I know you aren't dead. I hear you when I need to. I feel you when I need to. You are just a new form of life that I call upon whenever I need.

God is love, and you are love. No matter how "I'm the leader" Lil' Rall acts. Or how radical and adventurous Rasul's next project is. Or how many times Garrett Jedi-mind-tricks us into continuing to spoil him. Or how many times I cry, because it still doesn't take much. We will always have one another, and we will always love you because you truly have never left us. With your words, your wisdom, and your continued guidance as our ancestor, we will be okay.

You continue to give us the medicine that will one day heal all our wounds. We may be cut. We may be bruised. But because of you,

We. Are. Not. Broken.

14

We Are Not Broken

During the mid-'90s, the movie *Soul Food* hit the theaters. It was the must-see film for every Black person familiar with the ups and downs of the Black family experience. The story focused on this twelve-year-old Black boy and his family. He had three aunts, with his mother being the middle daughter, and they were led by "Big Mama," a matriarch who was like Nanny in many ways.

In the movie, Big Mama gets sick, and when she passes away, the family is broken apart. So, the twelve-year-old boy lies that Big Mama told him money was hidden in the house. Because of the fib, the family reunites for their regular Sunday dinner that Big Mama used to prepare before she died. In a surprise twist, Big Mama actually *did* hide money in the house, and the family came back together to love one another through it.

I decided to write this book on December 1, 2019. As you know it, Nanny died two days later. In many ways, I feared that everything Nanny had done to keep us together would fall apart, that we wouldn't be able to heal the brokenness from losing the largest presence in our lives. But instead of lying about hidden money, I took a different route. At that moment, I knew it would be necessary to tell our story to the world.

I go into every book with an idea of how it will look—from the chapters to the dedication, to the themes, to how I will synthesize them to all make sense. I always come out in the end with the book looking much different than it did when it began but always exactly what I need it to be.

For me, the phrase "we are not broken" speaks to the processes of heartbreak and healing. There are few times in my life when I felt my heart was broken. Nanny's passing was certainly one of those moments. I had built up an image of the future in my mind. As I watched her fight cancer, I just knew that once I made it to this place of success, she would have recovered enough to be my sidekick once again—like those days when I was by her side for every flea market and soup kitchen run. Her diagnosis could've broken me. It could've broken anyone, to be honest. But it didn't. In many ways it brought the family back together. In many ways we had to heal old trauma and start the conversations that we had put off for decades. We had to reach a place of peace with her, because we knew she wouldn't be comfortable to transition unless she was able to get it all off her mind and heart. In the end, while she was losing her life, she was healing all of ours.

This book is also a love letter to Blackness and the Black-boy experience. We got to be Black boys in totality and experience a wider world. When we consider the term "Black boy joy," what do we really mean? I think many people think so macro that they forget the magic in the small moments.

As someone who is extremely spiritual, I often think about the slave. Who were the slaves outside of their experience? Did the slave laugh? Did the slave cry? Did the slave look up at clouds and imagine? Did the slave daydream? Outside of their experience, what was their joy? Joy should have looked like liberation from the white master. Liberation from the existence that told them they were not human. Freedom from the constant abuses on their minds, bodies, and souls.

But joy could also look like the small moments. The moment in the field where two slaves in love caught each other's eyes. The moments when they were birthing their children and praying for a society that would one day be better for them. The moments when hopelessness became so great that they killed their masters, just for a taste of what freedom could hold.

I think about us as the descendants of them, dying under multiple systems of oppression. I think about us as Black boys birthed into these systems, systems that steal our childhood and, at times, our lives. But I also think about the joys. The joy of skipping rocks. The joy of heating up ice cream. The joy of riding bikes or flying kites in the midst of a world hell-bent on breaking us. It is in those moments of joy that we heal, even if slowly.

This book is also a love letter to centering Black people in Black stories, to tell our side outside white acceptance for validation. These are our truths—not just our trauma or bits and pieces of the puzzle but all the parts that make a beautiful image. There are so many stories we have. So. Many.

I think about the media portrayal of the Black boy in the hoodie. We were all the young Black boy in the hoodie. We are all the unarmed Black man who could be killed today or tomorrow. We are all just one interaction away from being the next trending hashtag. And although many of us navigate this space every day, we still laugh. Lil' Rall, Rasul, Garrett, and I were able to be creative and joyous Black boys—an experience that too many are often robbed of.

Most important, this book is an ode to the Black grandmothers who provide the tools necessary to navigate this anti-Black world. The Black grandmothers who feed us when we are hungry, clothe us when we are naked, and provide a roof over our head when we need to come out of the rain. The Black grandmothers who love us when we are great and love us even harder when we make mistakes.

Nanny gave so much of herself that there was often nothing left for her at the end of the night. She was self-sacrificing like her mother and the many Black women in her family before her. That should not be the requirement of the Black woman. When does the Black woman ever get to be free? I'm thankful that my Nanny had her Lord, because without it, some days I'm not sure if she felt she had anyone. People shouldn't have to leave the physical to get a taste of freedom, but I'm thankful she can be at peace in a place where cancer can no longer get to her.

We are descendants of the slave who died. A people they tried to break.

We are descendants of those who survived. A people they tried to break.

We are descendants of the slave who rebelled. A people they tried to break.

We are descendants of the strongest people on this planet. A people we are not ashamed of. A people we pull from spiritually. Nanny is now with those ancestors. And, like them, we will not break.

I leave you all with one final Nannyism: "It's a blessing in the water. Some people walk into the water and only get wet. Some people walk into the water and come out blessed." Her words are now the water for the world to walk into, and, like us, so many others will come out blessed.

We love you, Nanny.

Acknowledgments

You can never thank everyone but I'm certainly going to do my best to acknowledge those who played an important role in this journey of writing the hardest story in my life.

My family that continues to be the rock and foundation of my support. Thank you, Mommy and Daddy, for all that you've done and continue to do for me. Thank you to my siblings, Tonya, Gregory Jr., Garrett, and Brittany. Thank you to Aunt Munch, Aunt Sarah, Aunt Crystal, Aunt Darlene, and Aunt Audrey. Thank you, Uncle. You all have been so important in my life and I thank you for always having my best interests at heart. Thank you to everyone in the Johnson and Elder clan. I truly could not ask for a better family.

Thank you to my best friends Storm, Preston, and Rojan. For all the late-night phone calls and FaceTimes to help me navigate this thing called life. Thank you for your years of friendship and support that continues to be unflinching. I'm so grateful to have you all in my life and appreciate all that you do for me.

Thank you to my friends Rachel, Amanda, Sean, Kyle, Hari, Gabe, Mason, Shahem, and Twiggy. You all have become so important in my daily life. Each of you are very special to me and I don't take for granted any of the moments we get to share with each other. You are all more than my friends, you are truly my family.

Thank you to my line brothers from the Gamma Chapter of Alpha Phi Alpha Fraternity Incorporated. Fifteen years later and you all continue to be an important part of life. Special thanks to all of my Gamma Chapter brothers and many members of Alpha who continue to bless my life. '06!!!

Thank you to the "Fam." Fortunate that fifteen years later I still get to call you all friends and have your support in my life. May our group chat forever stay lit. You all keep me grounded and humbled and appreciative for every small moment.

Thank you to my "Village," my Black Queer circle, who I love dearly. You all continue to inspire me. You represent the best in created family.

Thank you to Nic Stone, for always being just a text

message away and for blurbing the book. Thank you, Aiden, Kiese, Mark, and Laurie, for your beautiful blurbs about the book. All of you truly make me feel affirmed.

Thank you to my film and TV team at the Gotham Group. Ellen for guiding me through this industry. Emily and Eitan and Dillon for all the work and support you put into my projects. Thank you to lawyer Anita, who has been a godsend in making sure I feel protected and knowledgeable about all the things I am working on. Thank you as well to my attorney Mark, who always advocates for better.

Thank you to my phenomenal agent Patrice Caldwell! Thank you for continuing to guide my career and help me dream the impossible dream and continue making the Black Art I wish I once had. Thank you to the amazing team at New Leaf Literary & Media. Special thanks to Jo and Joe Volpe for making me feel like I finally have a literary agency who truly cares for me and my career and fighting for what was right for me. Thank you to Hilary and Meredith as well for all the work they do for me.

Thank you to my team at LBYR. My editor Alexandra Hightower for allowing me to put this work in the world and being kind and guiding with this powerful story. Thank you, Johnalynn Holland, for the beautiful cover. Thank you to the LBYR team across all departments for supporting this important book. Looking forward to creating many more with you all.

Thank you to Nanny's grandkids: Lil' Rall, Lil' Kevin, Rasul, Garrett, Justice, and Kennedy. Our story is now in the world just the way our Nanny would want it. Thank you for making me better and always having my front and back. Thank you for just being you.

Thank you to the ancestors. Specifically Old Daddy, Grandma Lula Mae, Uncle Horace, Grandma Mildred, and my favorite girl. Our favorite girl. My Nanny.

VINCENT MARC

GEORGE M. JOHNSON

George M. Johnson is an award-winning Black nonbinary writer and activist based in the New York City area. As a journalist, George has written for major and niche media outlets on topics including race, gender, sex, HIV, intersectionality, politics, culture, health, and pop culture. They are the author of the bestselling memoir *All Boys Aren't Blue*. They invite you to visit them online at iamgmjohnson.com and on Twitter @IamGMJohnson.